The
Clean Eating
WITH STEAM
COOKBOOK

101 Surprisingly Delicious, Low-Fat, High-Nutrition Recipes for Modern Electric Food Steamers

By

KRISTIN AMBER

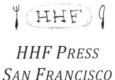

HHF Press
San Francisco

Editor: HHF Press

Art Direction: HHF Press

Illustrations: HHF Press

All photographs in this book © HHF Press or © Depositphotos.com

Published in the United States of America by HHF Press

www.HHFPress.com

Disclaimer:

Contents

CHAPTER

1

The Health Benefits
of Steaming Your Meals

Keep Nutrients Better Than Other Cooking Options

One of the biggest benefits of steaming foods, especially vegetables, is that this method keeps important vitamins inside the food instead of cooking it out. Eating steamed vegetables is the best way to get your essential vitamins from foods without missing out on taste. Broccoli, for example, keeps upwards of 80 percent of its Vitamin C content when steamed versus a measly 3% when microwaved. More importantly, you get these health benefits without having to compromise on the taste and texture of your food.

No Need to Add Oil or Other Unhealthy Additives

Oil adds calories and, depending on the type of oil, can be an unhealthy additive to food. The same goes for many other products that we add to foods to help them bake, fry, or grill. Steaming only needs all natural water to get the job done and the best part is, you don't lose out on any of the taste.

Preserves the Integrity of Food and Fiber in Vegetables

There is no need to worry about your vegetables turning into mash like some other cooking methods. This, again, means that you are getting more of the nutrients held within the food but it also has another important benefit. When vegetables are steamed, they keep all of the fiber locked within. Fiber is not only helpful in keeping your regular and fending off digestive problems, but it is also heart healthy.

No Smoke, No Smell, and No Burned Foods

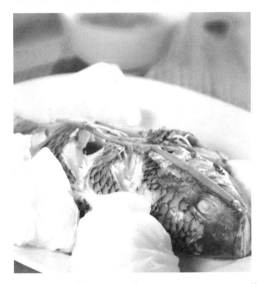

Other cooking methods can cause all kinds of problems for susceptible individuals. People with lung problems can be effected by too much smoke from foods and anyone with a weak stomach may lose it with the aroma released by other cooking methods. There is also no chance of burning foods, which some scientists believe that eating burnt meats can release free radicals in the body.

Steamed Food Digests Easier

Since steamed foods are already softened, they are easier for the body to break down and digest. Easy digestion leads to less indigestion and bloating, but it has an even more important benefit. Foods that are broken down faster make it easier for the body to absorb more of the key nutrients that are held within those foods.

2

How to Use
Your Food Steamer
Like an Expert

Easy Access Steaming Chart

The following is a quick list of commonly steamed foods. No need to waste your time looking up each food individually. Acorn Squash: 10 Minutes

- Artichokes: 5 Minutes
- Asparagus: 7 Minutes
- Beats: 24 Minutes
- Bell Peppers: 4 Minutes
- Broccoli: 12 Minutes
- Brussels Sprouts: 10 Minutes
- Butternut Squash: 10 Minutes
- Carrots: 15 Minutes
- Cauliflower: 12 Minutes
- Edamame: 5 Minutes
- Eggplant: 8 Minutes
- Corn on the Cob: 8 Minutes
- Green Beans: 10 Minutes
- Mushrooms: 5 Minutes

- Sliced Onion Rings: 5 Minutes
- Pearl Onions: 8 Minutes
- Whole Potatoes: 16 Minutes
- Spaghetti Squash: 22 Minutes
- Spinach: 7 Minutes
- Sugar Snap Peas: 5 Minutes
- Sweet Potatoes: 16 Minutes
- Tomatoes: 7 Minutes
- Yellow Squash: 8 Minutes
- Zucchini: 9 Minutes

Understanding and Using the Digital Touch Pad

We live in a digital age, so understanding the touch pad should be fairly easy, but we will break it down briefly. First, on the left hand side of the front you will see a small window that shows your water levels, always check your water levels before you start the machine. In case you forget, that is ok because this steamer has an indicator light that will inform you if your water level is getting too low. There are also three other lights that let you know if it is set to delay, cooking, or on warm mode. Delay can be set by pressing the delay button and pushing the arrows up or down to delay the start time. The buttons are also used to set your cook time for immediate steaming. Remember that you are delaying the start time, not setting a timer. Of course, the power button is also centered in the front of the machine. The digital read out is nicely backlit and easy to read so you will have no problem setting your time without error.

Understand the Function of Each Tier and Know When to Remove the Divider

The first tier is designed for smaller amounts of food; this is the perfect size for steaming your sides like vegetables and potatoes. If you add the second tier to cook a full meal you will want to move your proteins to the lower bowl and put the vegetables in the upper bowl. If the food you are cooking in the top bowl takes the same amount of time to cook as the bottom bowl you will want to give the food in the upper bowl an extra 5 minutes to cook since it takes the steam longer to get to it. If the food in the top bowl takes a shorter period to cook, you can always add the top bowl later in the cooking process. When you are steaming large foods like corn on the cob or an entire head of broccoli or cauliflower, you can remove the divider between the bowls to create one super steaming bowl.

Proper Cleaning and Storage of the Unit

Cleaning the device is simple, even though it doesn't fit in most dishwashers. The first thing you want to do is make sure that the steamer is unplugged, otherwise the results could be a bit shocking. Smaller pieces like the drip pan and rice bowl can be washed in the dishwasher. For bigger bowls, you can wash them with a sponge and dish soap in the sink and allow to air dry. You can also wipe down the inside and outside of the appliance with a damp (not soaking) towel. When it comes time to store it, the unique nested design makes this steamer compact enough to fit in a cupboard.

Proper Serving of Steamed Foods

One of the biggest problems with steamed food is that it loses its heat really fast, so it is a good idea to only remove it from the streamer right before your meal. For the best results you may even want to warm your plates up in the oven before serving to help keep the food warm. It may also be a good idea to pat down or drain some of the foods before serving in order to remove excess moisture from the food.

Proper Storage of Steamed Foods

The great thing about steamed foods is that there is not a lot of special care needed when storing them. For the most part steamed foods can be stored in the refrigerator in glass or plastic containers with airtight lids. Freezer storage works with freezer bags, just be sure that they are air tight in order to prevent freezer burn. Unlike other leftovers that can be compromised by condensation, it is actually beneficial for steamed foods so they can be stored warm. When reheating stored steamed foods, the microwave is your best bet. Don't be afraid to sprinkle some water over foods before microwaving to avoid the food drying out during reheating.

3

Pro Tips

Adding Wine and Spirits

Everything is better with wine including steaming. There are many gourmet recipes which call for the use of wine and spirits and cooking with a steamer is no different. Adding a little wine or otherwise indicated spirit is a great way to add a unique flavor to any dish. Just be aware that contrary to popular belief, not all alcohol is burned off in the cooking process which could be concerning to recovering alcoholics or discerning parents

Add Flavor, Herbs, and Aromatics Straight to the Water

Placing additives on the food is a great way to add flavor to a dish, but adding them to the water you steam the flavors right through the foods. Whatever the recipe calls for, experiment with adding

it straight into the water to see how much it changes the flavor profile. Be sure to empty the water and clean the reservoir after use so nothing stays behind to go bad.

Choose the Best Cuts of Meat and Freshest Fruits and Vegetables for The Best Taste Profile

This is true in every cooking method, but can be especially true when it comes to steaming. Choosing the best meats is important to the flavor, but choosing the best vegetables is important to the nutrition. The best fruits and vegetables will come straight from your back yard, but if you can't garden try to pick them up from a local farmers' market. The fresher the fruits and vegetables, the more nutrient packed they will be.

Always Cook Food in a Single Layer with Space in Between

Steaming may be a unique way to cook foods, but it is still susceptible to some of the main obstacles to cooking. Stacking foods on top of each other means that the stacked surfaces will most likely not be cooked thoroughly and packing foods close together means that the edges won't get cooked. At the very least cook times are going to take much longer than they should.

Meats and Juicy Foods Always Go on The Bottom

When you use a two tier system, there are some challenges that you are going to have to face. When you are steaming an entire meal, always make sure that you place any meats in the first tier. Not only do meats need to cook more thoroughly for food safety, but they also tend to drip as they cook. Instead of your other foods being covered in blood and other juices it becomes the drip pan's problem.

Always Let Foods in the Upper Tier Cook Longer

Food in the upper bowl will always take longer to cook because it is higher and the steam is being blocked by food in the bottom bowl. Always add at least 5 minutes onto the cook time of the top bowl to ensure that the food is cooked throughout. If the food usually takes a shorter amount of time to steam, you should be able to keep cook times the same.

Kristin Amber

CHAPTER

4

Steamed
Vegetable Recipes

Baby Corn and Mushroom Curry Rice

Serves: 4 | Prep Time: 15 Minutes | Cook Time: 8 Minutes

This one takes some unusual ingredients, but you will like it so much that the ingredients may become commonplace in your home.

Ingredients:

1/4 cup diagonally cut baby corn

1/4 cup sliced mushrooms

3 cups cooked long grained rice

1/2 cup coconut milk

1 1/2 teaspoons red curry paste

1/4 cup boiled green peas

10 diagonally cut french beans

1/4 teaspoon grated lemon rind

1 tablespoon finely chopped basil leaves

1 banana leaf, approx. 2" x 2"

Salt to taste

Instructions:

1. Put all of the ingredients, except the banana leaf, in a large bowl and mix well until combined evenly.

2. Lay the banana leaf on a flat surface and spoon the rice onto the middle of the leaf.

3. Fold each side of the banana leaf into the center to create a steaming packet and seal with a tooth pick.

4. Steam for 8 minutes, remove and serve immediately.

Nutritional Info: Calories: 646 | Sodium: 112 mg | Dietary Fiber: 6.7 g | Total Fat: 9.0 g | Total Carbs: 125.1 g | Protein: 14.1 g.

Steamed Brussels Sprouts

Servings: 12 | Prep Time: 3 Minutes | Cook Time: 8 Minutes

Brussels sprouts may be an acquired taste, but this recipe goes a long way to help curb the earthy taste.

Ingredients:

3 pounds small or medium brussels sprouts

Salt and pepper to taste

3 tablespoons unsalted butter

2 tablespoons finely chopped fresh chives

Instructions:

1. Soften butter, you can even melt the butter if you want.
2. Steam the sprouts for 8 minutes until soft.
3. Add sprouts to bowl with butter, salt, pepper, and chives.
4. Toss the ingredients together and serve.

Nutritional Info: Calories: 224 | Sodium: 146 mg | Dietary Fiber: 12.8 g | Total Fat: 9.8 g | Total Carbs: 31.0 g | Protein: 11.7 g.

Steamed Corn on the Cob

Servings: 12 | Prep Time: 5 Minutes | Cook Time: 15 Minutes

There is not a lot to this, but it is a great reminder that you can even prepare something as tough as corn in your steamer.

Ingredients:

12 ears of corn

Salt and pepper to taste

Instructions:

1. Husk corn and place in the steamer vertically.
2. Steam for 15 minutes.
3. Sprinkle with salt and pepper and serve.

Nutritional Info: Calories: 59 | Sodium: 13 mg | Dietary Fiber: 1.7 g | Total Fat: 0.5 g | Total Carbs: 14.1 g | Protein: 1.9 g.

Kristin Amber

Chinese Steamed Tofu

Servings: 2 | Prep Time: 5 Minutes | Cook Time: 5 Minutes

One of the many qualities of tofu is that it can be prepared in endless ways. This particular recipe brings some eastern flavor to your table.

Ingredients:

1 (14-ounce) block tofu	2 tablespoons canola oil
1 scallion	1 tablespoon soy sauce
2 cloves garlic	1 tablespoon sweet soy sauce

Instructions:

1. Slice greens of scallion into ribbons and thinly slice white parts.

2. Mince garlic and set aside.

3. Place the tofu on a small steam proof plate and steam for 5 minutes.

4. Drain as much excess liquid from the plate as possible.

5. In a microwave safe bowl combine oil and garlic and microwave for 3 minutes or until the garlic starts to brown.

6. Add soy sauces to the garlic and mix well.

7. Place scallions on top of tofu and drizzle with garlic sauce.

8. Serve immediately.

Nutritional Info: Calories: 278 | Sodium: 927 mg | Dietary Fiber: 2.2 g | Total Fat: 22.3 g | Total Carbs: 6.1 g | Protein: 17.6 g.

Bok Choy with Miso Lime Sauce

Servings: 4 | Prep Time: 10 Minutes | Cook Time: 5 Minutes

Since bok choy doesn't have a very bold taste to begin with it is important to pair it up with a sauce that can really bring out its flavor.

Ingredients:

2 1/2 tablespoons sake or dry sherry

1 teaspoons sugar

2 tablespoons white miso paste

1 teaspoon soy sauce

1 tablespoon lime juice

2 bunches baby bok choy

Sea salt to taste

Instructions:

1. Boil sake in a small sauce pan for 5 minutes to diminish the alcohol content.

2. Add the sugar and stir until dissolved, then turn to low heat.

3. Add miso paste and soy sauce and stir until mixed thoroughly.

4. Stir in lime juice, the sauce should be thick, but if it is too thick you can add a little water.

5. Steam the bok choy for 5 minutes.

6. Transfer to a plate and pour the sauce over the bok choy; serve immediately.

Nutritional Info: Calories: 85 | Sodium: 888 mg | Dietary Fiber: 2.5 g | Total Fat: 1.3 g | Total Carbs: 10.8 g | Protein: 4.5 g.

Butter Steamed New Potatoes

Servings: 4 | Prep Time: 5 Minutes | Cook Time: 12 Minutes

This southern style recipe is so simple yet bursting with flavor. Just writing this recipe down is giving me a craving for it.

Ingredients:

2 pounds of new or very small red potatoes

1/2 cup of butter

1/4 cup of water

1 teaspoon salt

1/2 teaspoon of black pepper

1/4 cup of chopped fresh parsley, loosely packed

Instructions:

1. In a medium sauce pan over medium heat, combine butter, water, salt, and pepper.
2. Scrub the potatoes and peel away a strip down the center of the potatoes.
3. Place the potatoes in a large bowl and pour the butter mix over the potatoes, toss to coat.
4. Remove potatoes from bowl and set aside the bowl with excess butter mix.
5. Steam potatoes for 12 minutes.
6. Transfer to a plate, pour extra butter over potatoes, top with parsley, and serve.

Nutritional Info: Calories: 364 | Sodium: 761 mg | Dietary Fiber: 4.0 g | Total Fat: 23.4 g | Total Carbs: 36.5 g | Protein: 4.7 g.

Carrot Dumplings

Serves: 10 | Prep Time: 20 Minutes | Cook Time: 12 Minutes

They are easy to make though they do take a little more time than some other sides.

Ingredients:

45 dumpling wrappers

1 pound carrots

1 cup dried shiitake mushrooms

4 cloves garlic

2 slices ginger

3 tablespoons sesame oil

3 large eggs, beaten

1 cup bamboo shoots, minced

1/4 teaspoon white pepper powder

1 tablespoon light soy sauce

1/2 teaspoon salt

Instructions:

1. Place mushrooms in a bowl with water and cover, let sit for 30 minutes while they rehydrate.
2. Drain the mushrooms and set them aside.
3. Put carrots, mushrooms, garlic, and ginger into a food processor and process until all the foods are minced.
4. Heat to tablespoons of oil over medium heat and add carrot mix, cook for about 5 minutes.
5. Move the carrot mix to a plate and allow to cool.
6. Beat eggs in a shallow bowl.
7. Add remaining oil to the same skillet and add eggs, cook until scrambled and break into small pieces.
8. Transfer eggs to another plate to cool.
9. In a large bowl mix carrot mix and eggs together along with white pepper powder, soy sauce, and salt.
10. Remove the wonton wrappers from the package and cover with a damp cloth.
11. One at a time, brush the edges of the wrapper with water and spoon 1/2 teaspoon of the carrot mix into the center.
12. Close the wrapper and set on a baking sheet, cover with a damp cloth.
13. Repeat until all of your wrappers are filled.
14. Spray the bottom of your steamer bowl with vegetable spray.
15. Place as many wrappers as you can in the bowl with a little space between each one.
16. Steam for 12 minutes and serve immediately.

Nutritional Info: Calories: 513 | Sodium: 1094 mg | Dietary Fiber: 4.5 g |
Total Fat: 7.9 g | Total Carbs: 92.1 g | Protein: 17.2 g.

Kristin Amber

Jamaican Steamed Carrot and Cabbage

Servings: 4 | Prep Time: 15 Minutes | Cook Time: 15 Minutes

This is a fun side that you don't see all of the time. It is an excellent recipe to serve with chicken, especially jerked chicken.

Ingredients:

1 cabbage	1/8 teaspoon allspice
2 carrots	1 teaspoon salt
1/2 cup bell pepper	1 teaspoon pepper
1 onion	1/4 cup water
1 garlic clove	1/2 scotch bonnet pepper
2 tablespoons oil	

Instructions:

1. Chop cabbage, peppers, and onion; mince garlic and grate the carrots.

2. Add oil to a pan and sauté onions and peppers for about 5 minutes.

3. Mix in the garlic and sauté for another 5 minutes.

4. Mix carrot and cabbage into a medium bowl, then add pepper mix.

5. Sprinkle allspice, salt, and pepper over the mixture.

6. Mix thoroughly and place in steamer bowl.

7. Steam for 15 minutes and serve.

Nutritional Info: Calories: 137 | Sodium: 637 mg | Dietary Fiber: 6.3 g |
Total Fat: 7.1 g | Total Carbs: 17.7 g | Protein: 3.2 g.

Steamed Asparagus

Servings: 4 | Prep Time: 5 Minutes | Cook Time: 10 Minutes

Sometimes simple is better as shown by this 3-ingredient recipe.

Ingredients:

1 bunch asparagus

2 teaspoons butter

1/4 teaspoon salt

Instructions:

1. Steam asparagus for 10 minutes.
2. Soften or melt butter while asparagus steams.
3. Add asparagus, butter, and salt to a bowl and toss.
4. Serve immediately.

Nutritional Info: Calories: 37 | Sodium: 163 mg | Dietary Fiber: 2.1 g | Total Fat: 2.0 g | Total Carbs: 3.9 g | Protein: 2.2 g.

Steamed Broccoli

Serves: 4 | Prep Time: 5 Minutes | Cook Time: 12 Minutes

This recipe keeps it simple, but adds a little pizzazz to an otherwise boring vegetable.

Ingredients:

1 head of broccoli

1 lemon

Fresh black pepper

Instructions:

1. Cut the crowns from the stem and break them into florets.
2. Cut lemons into quarters.
3. Place the florets into the steamer bowl.
4. Squeeze lemon over broccoli then sprinkle with pepper.
5. Steam for 12 minutes.

Nutritional Info: Calories: 23 | Sodium: 19 mg | Dietary Fiber: 1.9 g | Total Fat: 0.2 g | Total Carbs: 5.1 g | Protein: 1.7 g.

Kristin Amber

French Potato Salad

Serves: 4 | Prep Time: 20 Minutes | Cook Time: 10 Minutes

Potato salad is a classic dish that goes with so many entrees, especially in the summertime.

Ingredients:

1 pound small white boiling potatoes

1 pound small red boiling potatoes

2 tablespoons good dry white wine

2 tablespoons chicken stock

3 tablespoons champagne vinegar

1/2 teaspoon Dijon mustard

2 teaspoons kosher salt

3/4 teaspoons freshly ground black pepper

10 tablespoons good olive oil

1/4 cup minced scallions

2 tablespoons minced fresh dill

2 tablespoons minced flat-leaf parsley

2 tablespoons julienned fresh basil leave

Instructions:

1. Steam your potatoes for 16 minutes, you may have to remove the divider to fit them all in.

2. Set the potatoes aside until they are cool enough to handle.

3. Halve each potato width wise and put them in a medium bowl.

4. Pour wine and chicken stock over potatoes and toss to coat, set aside and let soak.

5. In a separate bowl, combine the vinegar, mustard, 1/2 teaspoon salt, and 1/4 teaspoon pepper together.

6. Slowly stir in the olive oil to create a vinaigrette.

7. Pour the vinaigrette over the potatoes and toss gently.

8. Add basil, parsley, dill, scallions, 1 1/2 teaspoons of salt, and 1/2 teaspoon of pepper and toss gently a few more times.

9. Serve at room temperature.

Nutritional Info: Calories: 476 | Sodium: 1207 mg | Dietary Fiber: 5.3 g |
Total Fat: 35.5 g | Total Carbs: 38.1 g | Protein: 4.7 g.

Mashed Cauli-tatoes

Servings: 2 | Prep Time: 5 Minutes | Cook Time: 15 Minutes

This is seriously an awesome side, you get all of the texture of mashed potatoes with half the carbs and calories.

Ingredients:

1 large head fresh cauliflower

3 tablespoons butter

1 teaspoon sea salt

1 teaspoon garlic powder

1/2 teaspoon black pepper

Fresh herbs of your choice, such as parsley or chives

Instructions:

1. Chop off the stems of the cauliflower, then chop the florets into tiny pieces.
2. Steam cauliflower for 12 minutes.
3. Transfer the cauliflower to a blender.
4. Add butter and blend for another 30 seconds.
5. Sprinkle with your chopped herbs and serve.

Nutritional Info: Calories: 264 | Sodium: 1185 mg | Dietary Fiber: 10.8 g | Total Fat: 17.7 g | Total Carbs: 23.6 g | Protein: 8.8 g.

Quick Steamed Carrots

Servings: 1 | Prep Time: 10 Minutes | Cook Time: 2 Minutes

This super-fast side is not only good in a pinch but it also takes steamed carrots and makes them something more than just steamed vegetables.

Ingredients:

1 cup baby carrots

2 teaspoons orange juice

2 teaspoons honey

1 dash ground ginger

Instructions:

1. Place your carrots in the steamer and steam for 10 minutes.
2. Place carrots, juice, honey, and ginger in a bowl and toss.
3. Serve this sweet treat warm.

Nutritional Info: Calories: 129 | Sodium: 180 mg | Dietary Fiber: 6.8 g | Total Fat: 0.3 g | Total Carbs: 31.7 g | Protein: 1.6 g.

Simple Steamed Sweet Potatoes

Servings: 4 | Prep Time: 12 Minutes | Cook Time: 2 Minutes

It's not just that sweet potatoes are perfect for a steamer, but they are also a healthy alternative to many other sides.

Ingredients:

1 pound sweet potatoes	2 shallots
2 cloves garlic	1 teaspoon cinnamon
3 tablespoons walnut oil	1/4 teaspoon nutmeg
2 tablespoons sesame seeds	1/4 teaspoon cloves
2 tablespoons fresh rosemary	Salt and white pepper to taste

Instructions:

1. Cut sweet potatoes into 1-inch cubes, mince garlic, and chop shallots.

2. Steam the sweet potatoes, shallots, and garlic for 12 minutes.

3. Transfer the steamed vegetables to a large mixing bowl and combine the rest of the ingredients in the bowl.

4. Toss the ingredients together and serve.

Nutritional Info: Calories: 235 | Sodium: 17 mg | Dietary Fiber: 6.7 g | Total Fat: 6.3 g | Total Carbs: 42.2 g | Protein: 5.2 g.

Sautéed Bacon and Steamed String Beans

Servings: 4 | Prep Time: 10 Minutes | Cook Time: 5 Minutes

Beware! when the rest of the family smells what you are cooking, they may start pushing you to get dinner done sooner.

Ingredients:

1 tablespoon olive oil

6 strips bacon

1 cup thinly sliced onion

2 tablespoons sliced garlic

2 pounds string beans

1 teaspoon salt

1/2 teaspoon black pepper

Instructions:

1. Cook bacon and chop into 1/2-inch pieces.

2. Put olive oil in a pan over medium heat and add bacon.

3. Cook bacon for about 5 minutes, then add onions and garlic for another 5 minutes.

4. While the bacon and vegetables cook, steam your string beans for 5 minutes.

5. Pour beans into a large bowl, then pour bacon mix on top.

6. Add salt and pepper and stir until beans are coated with bacon and serve.

Nutritional Info: Calories: 273 | Sodium: 1255 mg | Dietary Fiber: 8.5 g | Total Fat: 15.7 g | Total Carbs: 20.8 g | Protein: 15.3 g.

Kristin Amber

Steamed Edamame

Servings: 2 | Prep Time: 1 Minute | Cook Time: 5 Minutes

This vegetable has been growing in popularity as a side and simple recipes like this prove why.

Ingredients:

2 cups fresh edamame

1 tablespoon sea salt

Instructions:

1. Steam edamame for 5 minutes.
2. Transfer to bowl and toss with sea salt.
3. Serve warm.

Nutritional Info: Calories: 376 | Sodium: 2846 mg | Dietary Fiber: 10.8 g | Total Fat: 17.4 g | Total Carbs: 28.3 g | Protein: 33.1 g.

Turned Steamed Potatoes

Servings: 2 | Prep Time: 10 Minutes | Cook Time: 20 Minutes

Potatoes and steamers are made for each other and this is another simple recipe that makes that fact abundantly clear.

Ingredients:

7 small yellow potatoes
1 tablespoon butter

2 tablespoons chopped fresh herbs
1/4 teaspoon white pepper

Instructions:

1. Peel potatoes, rotating as you go to create a football like shape.
2. Steam potatoes for 20 minutes.
3. Pour potatoes into a large bowl.
4. Add butter, herbs, and pepper, toss to coat.
5. Serve warm.

Nutritional Info: Calories: 465 | Sodium: 77 mg | Dietary Fiber: 14.8 g | Total Fat: 6.4 g | Total Carbs: 94.4 g | Protein: 10.3 g.

Steamed Enoki Mushrooms

Servings: 1 | Prep Time: 5 Minutes | Cook Time: 6 Minutes

This recipe is a fun way to spice up a meal and would pair well with some savory steak.

Ingredients:

150g fresh enoki mushrooms

1 teaspoon sesame oil

1 green onion

5 garlic cloves

1 tablespoon cooking oil

1/8 teaspoon sugar

1 tablespoon light soy sauce

Pinch of salt

Instructions:

1. Remove hard ends from enoki and wash.

2. Mince garlic cloves.

3. Steam enoki for six minutes.

4. While the enoki steams, heat oil over medium heat and add garlic, sauté for about 3 minutes then remove from heat.

5. Add sugar, salt, and soy sauce and mix well.

6. Chop green onions.

7. Transfer enoki to a plate and top with green onions and garlic sauce.

Nutritional Info: Calories: 257 | Sodium: 667 mg | Dietary Fiber: 4.8 g |
Total Fat: 18.7 g | Total Carbs: 20.2 g | Protein: 5.5 g.

Kristin Amber

Steamed Leeks with Mustard-Shallot Vinaigrette

Servings: 4 | Prep Time: 15 Minutes | Cook Time: 10 Minutes

It sounds delicious, but it tastes even better and it is an excellent side to impress guests at a dinner party.

Ingredients:

2 large leeks	1 teaspoon balsamic vinegar
1 small shallot	1/4 cup extra-virgin olive oil
1 tablespoon Dijon mustard	Salt and pepper to taste
1 tablespoon red wine vinegar	1 tablespoon chopped parsley

Instructions:

1. Cut leaks into 2 x 2 1/2-inch strips and mince shallot.
2. Steam leaks for 5 minutes then place them on a plate covered in paper towels and refrigerate for 10 minutes.
3. While the leaks cool combine vinegars, mustard, and shallot in a small bowl.
4. Mix in olive oil slowly and sprinkle with salt and pepper.
5. Place the leaks on a plate in a triangular pile.
6. Drizzle the vinegar mix over the mound and sprinkle with parsley.

Nutritional Info: Calories: 195 | Sodium: 24 mg | Dietary Fiber: 2.5 g |
Total Fat: 13.8 g | Total Carbs: 18.0 g | Protein: 2.6 g.

Steamed Pumpkin and Baby Bok Choy with Ginger Sesame Sauce Recipe

Servings: 4 | Prep Time: 10 Minutes | Cook Time: 10 Minutes

This fall recipe proves that you can make a gourmet side out of anything.

Ingredients:

2 tablespoons olive oil

2 teaspoons toasted sesame oil

3 tablespoons coconut aminos

1-inch piece of peeled fresh ginger

1 to 2 garlic cloves

A pinch of red pepper flakes

4 heads baby bok choy

1 small kuri pumpkin

1 tablespoon toasted sesame seeds

Instructions:

1. Grate ginger and mince garlic.

2. In a medium sauce pan, combine sesame oil, olive oil, coconut aminos, ginger, garlic, and a pinch of red pepper flakes. Heat over medium heat for 5 minutes then cover and set aside.

3. Quarter the bok choy and peel, seed, and slice pumpkin.

4. Place the pumpkin in the bottom bowl of your steamer and bok choy in the top bowl and steam for 10 minutes.

5. Combine both onto a plate, drizzle with ginger mix, top with sesame seeds, and serve.

Nutritional Info: Calories: 237 | Sodium: 562 mg | Dietary Fiber: 10.3 g |
Total Fat: 12.3 g | Total Carbs: 26.5 g | Protein: 13.8 g.

Steamed Scallion Buns

Servings: 5 | Prep Time: 1 hour 30 Minutes | Cook Time: 20 Minutes

This recipe is not exactly simple, but the end results are totally worth it.

Ingredients:

2 1/2 cups all-purpose flour
Pinch of salt
3/4 cups water
1 1/2 teaspoons instant yeast

1 cup finely chopped scallion
Olive oil for brushing
Chinese 5 spice powder

Instructions:

1. Add flour, yeast, salt, and water to a bowl and mix into a dough.

1. Knead the dough by hand until smooth and then cover and set aside for 1 hour.

2. After an hour, the dough should have doubled in size, remove from bowl and divide into 2 equal halves.

3. Roll one half of the dough into a rectangle. Brush with oil and sprinkle with salt and Chinese spice.

4. Dump scallions across the rectangle and roll it up tightly. Cut into 10 equal portions. Repeat with other half of the dough.

5. Overlay two pieces together and press down in the middle to combine the two.

6. Grab each sides and fold the ends under. Line your steamer with parchment paper and place the buns on the paper. Steam for 20 minutes.

Nutritional Info: Calories: 237 | Sodium: 6 mg | Dietary Fiber: 2.5 g |
Total Fat: 0.7 g | Total Carbs: 49.6 g | Protein: 7.3 g.

Steamed Spinach with Herbs

Servings: 4 | Prep Time: 2 Minutes | Cook Time: 5 Minutes

Popeye wishes that his spinach would taste this good. This is a quick recipe and tastes good enough that the kids may even like it.

Ingredients:

2 (10-ounce) bags of fresh spinach	Salt and pepper to taste
1 cup fresh chopped parsley	Lemon wedge
1/4 cup sherry wine vinegar	

Instructions:

1. Combine spinach and parsley in a bowl and pour it into the steamer bowl.
2. Steam for 5 minutes.
3. Place on a serving plate and drizzle with vinegar.
4. Sprinkle with salt and pepper.
5. Squeeze lemon over and serve.

Nutritional Info: Calories: 53 | Sodium: 494 mg | Dietary Fiber: 3.6 g |
Total Fat: 0.7 g | Total Carbs: 10.0 g | Protein: 4.5 g.

Steamed Spinach with Lemon

Servings: 4 | Prep Time: 1 Minutes | Cook Time: 3 Minutes

Spinach in a steamer is so easy and possibly one of the healthiest vegetables you can make in a steamer.

Ingredients:

9 ounces baby or trimmed regular spinach	1 tablespoon fresh lemon juice, plus lemon wedges for garnish
1 tablespoon extra-virgin olive oil	1/8 teaspoon salt

Instructions:

1. Place spinach in the steamer and steam for three minutes.
2. Transfer to a bowl and add oil, lemon juice, and salt.
3. Toss to coat then serve with lemon wedges.

Nutritional Info: Calories: 46 | Sodium: 125 mg | Dietary Fiber: 1.4 g |
Total Fat: 3.8 g | Total Carbs: 2.4 g | Protein: 1.9 g.

Kristin Amber

Steamed Squash

Servings: 4 | Prep Time: 10 minutes | Cook Time: 10 minutes

Squash is basically made for a food steamer. The trick is to dress it up to make it more than just another steamed squash dish.

Ingredients:

1 pound yellow squash

1 sweet onion

2 tablespoons butter

1/2 teaspoon seasoned pepper

1 teaspoon sugar

Instructions:

1. Slice squash into 1/2-inch-thick strips and chop onion.

2. Put squash and onion in a bowl and toss together.

3. Pour into the steamer and steam for 10 minutes.

4. Pour back into bowl and mix in butter, sugar, and pepper.

5. Serve immediately.

Nutritional Info: Calories: 84 | Sodium: 53 mg | Dietary Fiber: 1.9 g |
Total Fat: 6.0 g | Total Carbs: 7.5 g | Protein: 1.8 g.

Steamed Sweet Potatoes with Wild Rice, Basil, and Tomato Chili Sauce

Servings: 2 | Prep Time: 1 Hour 5 Minutes | Cook Time: 12 Minutes

The name makes this dish seem like it is complicated to make, but it is actually pretty simple and tastes amazing.

Ingredients:

1 tomato

1 tablespoon miso paste

1 tablespoon lemon juice

1 tablespoon maple syrup

1 teaspoon chili powder, to taste

1 garlic clove

1 large sweet potato, sliced and steamed until soft and tender

2 cups cooked wild rice

1/4 cup basil leaves

Instructions:

1. Start by cooking the wild rice as it can take upwards of an hour to cook.

2. Place every ingredient up to the sweet potatoes into a blender and blend until smooth.

3. Cut the potato into slices and steam for 12 minutes.

4. Mix sauce and rice together and add sweet potato slices.

5. Sprinkle basil over the dish and serve.

Nutritional Info: Calories: 710 | Sodium: 381 mg | Dietary Fiber: 14.3 g | Total Fat: 2.8 g | Total Carbs: 150.1 g | Protein: 27.1 g.

Steamed Tofu and Vegetables

Servings: 4 | Prep Time: 20 Minutes | Cook Time: 10 Minutes

This is an awesome recipe that can be used as a side or a main dish.

Ingredients:

1 or 2 blocks of tofu

1 ear of corn

3 spring onions

1/4 pound of sugar snap peas or pea pods

1/4 pound of baby asparagus

1/4 pound of shiitake mushrooms

1 small bunch of cilantro

1 piece of fresh ginger about 2-inch long

1 small clove of garlic

2 tablespoons of soy sauce

2 teaspoons chilies oil

1 teaspoons of sesame oil

1 teaspoon of vegetable oil

1 lime

Red chili flakes

Instructions:

1. Set a stack of paper towels on a plate and lay tofu on top.
2. Place a second plate on top of tofu and weigh it down (most people use a can of vegetables)
3. Shuck the corn and cut it into 1 inch rounds.
4. Slice spring onions into 1/2-inch pieces.
5. Chop cilantro and set aside all vegetables.
6. Slice lime in half and peel and slice ginger into match sticks.
7. Combine ginger, garlic, soy sauce, chili flakes, and oil in a bowl to create sauce.
8. Squeeze in lime juice and stir.
9. Place tofu on a steamer safe plate and add onions and corn.
10. Place the tofu plate in the bottom bowl and all other vegetable in the top bowl.
11. Steam for 8 minutes.
12. Combine tofu and veggies on a serving platter and pour dressing over.
13. Top with cilantro and chili flakes and serve.

Simple Steamed Artichokes

Servings: 4 | Prep Time: 10 minutes | Cook Time: 35 Minutes

Artichokes are a delicious vegetable that don't need much to go from ordinary to extraordinary.

Ingredients:

4 artichokes	3 lemon slices
1 bay leaf	Salt and pepper to taste
3 garlic cloves, crushed	

Instructions:

1. Wash the artichokes and cut off the stems.
2. Gently spread the leaves of the artichokes and lay them upside down in the steamer.
3. Place bay leaf, garlic, and lemons around the artichokes and sprinkle salt and pepper on top.
4. Steam for 35 minutes.

Nutritional Info: Calories: 82 | Sodium: 153 mg | Dietary Fiber: 9.0 g | Total Fat: 0.3 g | Total Carbs: 18.4 g | Protein: 5.5 g.

Steamed Potatoes with Butter and Herbs

Servings: 8 | Prep Time: 5 Minutes | Cook Time: 25 Minutes

Steaming potatoes is easy but making them magnificent takes a great recipe.

Ingredients:

2 pounds small unpeeled potatoes	2 1/2 tablespoons mixed fresh herbs (parsley, thyme, rosemary, etc.)
2 tablespoons unsalted butter at room temperature.	Salt to taste

Instructions:

1. Scrub your potatoes well. Place in your steamer and steam for about 20 minutes.
2. Warm a serving bowl in the microwave or the oven.
3. Place potatoes in the serving bowl and add butter and herbs.
4. Toss together, top with salt, and serve.

Nutritional Info: Calories: 105 | Sodium: 27 mg | Dietary Fiber: 2.9 g | Total Fat: 3.0 g | Total Carbs: 18.1 g | Protein: 2.0 g.

Kristin Amber

Steamed Vegetable Wontons

Servings: 6 | Prep Time: 15 Minutes | Cook Time: 10 minutes

This recipe is similar to a few others, but it has a more manageable yield for a smaller serving and is packed with more flavors than you can imagine.

Ingredients:

20 to 24 wonton wrappers

1 tablespoon cornstarch

1/4 cup water

1 cup cabbage, shredded

3 tablespoons freshly chopped scallion

1 cup grated carrot

1 cup white button mushrooms, diced

3 teaspoons fresh minced ginger

2 tablespoons soy sauce

1/2 tablespoon Sriracha

1 tablespoon hoisin sauce

1 tablespoon chopped cilantro leaves

1 teaspoon sesame oil

1 teaspoon salt

1/2 teaspoon pepper

Instructions:

1. Stir together shredded cabbage, scallion, grated carrot, mushrooms, 3 teaspoons minced ginger, 2 tablespoons soy sauce, Sriracha, hoisin, cilantro, sesame oil, salt and pepper in a large bowl.

2. Whisk together water and cornstarch in a small bowl.

3. Lay out wonton wrappers and brush all four edges with the starch water.

4. Place an overflowing teaspoon of the veggie mix into the center of wonton.

5. Fold the wonton in half to form a triangle, then fold each side over to enclose the veggie mix.

6. Place in steamer and steam for 10 minutes.

Nutritional Info: Calories: 412 | Sodium: 1489 mg | Dietary Fiber: 3.5 g |
Total Fat: 2.9 g | Total Carbs: 81.0 g | Protein: 13.8 g.

Vegan Dim Sum Buns

Servings: 8 | Prep Time: 25 Minutes | Cook Time: 12 Minutes

Just because someone is a vegan doesn't mean they should miss out on all the fun.

Instructions:

2 cloves of garlic	4 spring onions
1 thumb-sized piece of fresh ginger	1 fresh red chili
1/2 bunch of fresh coriander	1 tablespoon sesame oil
Groundnut oil	1 3/4 cups coconut milk
2 cups mixed mushrooms	2 heaping cups self-rising flour
2 tablespoons rice wine vinegar	Salt to taste
2 tablespoons sweet chili sauce	2 tablespoons sesame seeds
2 tablespoons low-salt soy sauce	

Instructions:

1. Peel and slice the ginger and garlic.
2. Remove coriander leaves and set aside, finely slice the stalks.
3. Throw a splash of groundnut oil in a pan and add garlic, ginger and coriander stalks. Sauté for 3 minutes.
4. Add mushrooms to the pan and sauté for another 5 minutes.
5. Add vinegar, soy, and chili sauce to the mix and sauté for an additional 5 minutes.
6. Transfer mushroom mix to a large bowl.
7. Trim and finely chop the spring onions, add the white parts to the bowl.
8. Finely slice chilies, removing any seeds, add half to the bowl and set aside the other half.
9. Add sesame oil to the bowl, stir all ingredients, and set aside.
10. In a separate bowl add milk, flour, and salt and beat into a dough.
11. Roll the dough into a thick log and cut into 12 equal pieces.
12. Roll the pieces into balls and then flatten them into circles.
13. Spoon equal parts of the mushroom mix into the center of each circle.
14. Fold the circle up and around the mixture, pinch together to seal.
15. Spray the bowl with cooking spray and place the buns in the bowl seam side down.
16. Steam for 12 minutes. While the buns steam, toast the sesame seeds.
17. When the buns are ready top with seeds and coriander leaves and serve.

Nutritional Info: Calories: 272 | Sodium: 268 mg | Dietary Fiber: 2.6 g |
Total Fat: 14.7 g | Total Carbs: 30.6 g | Protein: 5.5 g.

Kristin Amber

Veggie-Tofu Dumplings

Servings: 10 | Prep Time: 50 Minutes | Cook Time: 12 Minutes

Dumplings are delicious and when prepared properly, they make for a great side or an even better appetizer.

Ingredients:

1/2 pound firm tofu

1/2 cup coarsely grated carrots

1/2 cup shredded cabbage

2 tablespoons finely chopped red pepper

2 tablespoons finely chopped scallions

2 teaspoons finely minced fresh ginger

1 tablespoon chopped cilantro leaves

1 tablespoon soy sauce

1 tablespoon hoisin sauce

2 teaspoons sesame oil

1 egg, lightly beaten

1 teaspoon kosher salt

1/4 teaspoon freshly ground black pepper

35 to 40 small wonton wrappers

Non-stick vegetable spray, for the steamer

Instructions:

1. Preheat the oven to 200 degrees.
2. Cut the tofu in half horizontally and place on a plate covered in paper towels.
3. Put another layer of paper towels over the tofu and place another plate on top of those towels.
4. Weigh the top plate down, most people use a can of vegetables.
5. Let the tofu drain for about 20 minutes.
6. When the tofu is ready cut it into 1/4-inch cubes and put it in a medium mixing bowl.
7. Add the remaining ingredients to the bowl and stir lightly until the ingredients are even throughout.
8. Remove the wonton wrappers from the package and cover with a damp cloth.
9. One at a time, brussh the edges of the wrapper with water and spoon 1/2 teaspoon of the tofu mix into the center.
10. Close the wrapper and set on a baking sheet, cover with a damp cloth.
11. Repeat until all your wrappers are filled.
12. Spray the bottom of your steamer bowl with vegetable spray.
13. Place as many wrappers as you can in the bowl with a little space between each one.
14. Steam for 12 minutes and serve immediately, if you can't serve immediately, place in the oven to keep warm.

Nutritional Info: Calories: 413 | Sodium: 1094 mg | Dietary Fiber: 2.9 g | Total Fat: 4.3 g | Total Carbs: 76.6 g | Protein: 15.3 g.

Vegetarian Steam Dumplings 2

Servings: 10 | Prep Time: 5 Minutes | Cook Time: 12 Minutes

The great thing about dumpling is that you can pretty much put whatever you want in them.

Ingredients:

1/2 cup finely chopped mushrooms

1/2 cup grated carrots

1/2 cup shredded cabbage

2 tablespoons finely chopped red pepper

2 tablespoons finely chopped onion

2 teaspoons minced fresh ginger

1 tablespoon soy sauce

1 tablespoon sesame oil

Salt and pepper to taste

35-40 small dumpling wrappers

Instructions:

1. In a large bowl, mix together all ingredients except for wrappers.

2. Remove the wonton wrappers from the package and cover with a damp cloth.

3. One at a time, brush the edges of the wrapper with water and spoon 1/2 teaspoon of the tofu mix into the center.

4. Close the wrapper and set on a baking sheet, cover with a damp cloth.

5. Repeat until all your wrappers are filled.

6. Spray the bottom of your steamer bowl with vegetable spray.

7. Place as many wrappers as you can in the bowl with a little space between each one.

8. Steam for 12 minutes and serve immediately, if you can't serve immediately, place in the oven to keep warm.

Nutritional Info: Calories: 392 | Sodium: 827 mg | Dietary Fiber: 2.7 g |
Total Fat: 3.3 g | Total Carbs: 75.6 g | Protein: 12.9 g.

Kristin Amber

CHAPTER

5

Steamed
Fish and Seafood

Asian Style Steamed Shrimp and Mushroom Parcels

Servings: 4 | Prep Time: 45 Minutes | Cook Time: 20 Minutes

This recipe is relatively easy to prepare, but gives off the impression of much more difficult recipe.

Ingredients:

32-40 medium-sized raw shrimps, cleaned and deveined (8-10 shrimps per person, about 1-pound in all)	2 tablespoons tamarind juice
	1-inch piece ginger
1/4 teaspoon baking soda	2-3 spring onions, root trimmed and chopped roughly
8 large shiitake mushrooms	
4-6 teaspoons of green tea leaves	Handful of cilantro leaves
4 large pieces of parchment paper	2 tablespoons light soy sauce
2 tablespoons olive oil	4 tablespoons brown sugar
5 lemongrass stalks, white part only, sliced roughly	2 teaspoons ground coriander seed
	Salt to taste
1/2 tablespoon chili flakes	

Instructions:

1. Pat shrimp dry with a paper towel, then set aside in a large bowl.
2. Place all the ingredients from the lemongrass stalks down into a food processor and process into a paste.
3. Add olive oil and pulse until the mixture is smooth.
4. Add the baking soda to the marinade and mix well.
5. Pour the marinade over the shrimp and mix it in.
6. Cover the shrimp and set aside for 30 minutes to marinate.
7. Slice mushrooms into thick slices and set aside.
8. Lay out the parchment paper and sprinkle green tea leaves evenly over each piece.
9. Lay shrimp evenly over green tea leaves and place mushrooms next to the shrimp.
10. Pour the remaining marinade evenly over the 4 parcels.
11. Fold the edges of the parchment paper in, then folds the top and bottom in to create a packet.
12. Lay in the steamer and steam for 20 minutes, serve over rice.

Nutritional Info: Calories: 479 | Sodium: 1422 mg | Dietary Fiber: 4.1 g |
Total Fat: 11.4 g | Total Carbs: 42.5 g | Protein: 53.9 g.

Asian Style Salmon

Servings: 4 | Prep Time: 10 Minutes | Cook Time: 10 Minutes

This just one of many ways to prepare one of the most popular fish filets around.

Ingredients:

- 4 (6-ounce) salmon portions, skin off
- 2-inch piece fresh ginger, peeled & grated finely
- 1 lime, zested and juiced
- 4-inch piece lemongrass, finely chopped
- 1/4 teaspoon turmeric ground

- 1/2 teaspoon sesame oil
- 1/2 cup sweet chili sauce
- 1/4 cup soy sauce
- 2 teaspoons fish sauce
- 1 teaspoon sesame oil

Instructions:

1. Place the ginger, lime zest & juice, lemongrass, turmeric, and sesame oil into a food processor and process into a paste.

2. Spread the paste over each piece of salmon and lay the salmon on a square of parchment paper.

3. Steam for 8 minutes.

4. Place on a plate and drizzle sesame oil and, soy, chili, and fish sauces over before serving.

Nutritional Info: Calories: 331 | Sodium: 1447 mg | Dietary Fiber: 1.1 g |
Total Fat: 12.5 g | Total Carbs: 18.1 g | Protein: 34.7 g.

Coconut Poached Fish

Servings: 4 | Prep Time: 35 Minutes | Cook Time: 10 Minutes

The sweetness of the coconut sets off the taste of the fish for an incredibly unique flavor profile.

Ingredients:

1 1/2 cups coconut cream

Grated zest and juice of 1 lemon

1 tablespoon fish sauce

1 tablespoon brown sugar

2 teaspoons sambal oelek

1 garlic clove

4 (4-ounce) firm white fish fillets

1 cup baby spinach leaves

Steamed rice, to serve

Instructions:

1. Crush your garlic and steam rice according to instructions (20 – 30 Minutes).

2. Combine cream, lemon juice and zest, fish sauce, brown sugar, sambal oelek, and garlic. Mix together and bring to boil.

3. Add fish to the pan and reduce heat, simmering for about 10 minutes.

4. Remove fish and serve on steamed rice, top with spinach.

Nutritional Info: Calories: 424 | Sodium: 461 mg | Dietary Fiber: 2.8 g | Total Fat: 30.2 g | Total Carbs: 10.2 g | Protein: 30.6 g.

Lemony Steamed Fish

Servings: 6 | Prep Time: 10 Minutes | Cook Time: 12 Minutes

Lemon and fish naturally go together; this recipe cuts out the middle man so to say and comes prepare in lemon.

Ingredients:

6 (6-ounce) halibut fillets
1 tablespoon dried dill weed
1 tablespoon onion powder
2 teaspoons dried parsley
1/4 teaspoon paprika

1 pinch seasoned salt, or more to taste
1 pinch lemon pepper
1 pinch garlic powder
2 tablespoons lemon juice

Instructions:

1. Cut 6 foil squares large enough to wrap around the fish.
2. Place fillets at the center of the foil.
3. Sprinkle seasonings over each fillet.
4. Drip lemon juice over each fillet.
5. Fold up edges of foil and seal them to create a packet.
6. Steam for 12 minutes and serve.

Nutritional Info: Calories: 6769 | Sodium: 3352 mg | Dietary Fiber: 0 g | Total Fat: 142.5 g | Total Carbs: 1.5 g | Protein: 1286.7 g.

Salmon and Enoki Mushroom Steamed Rice Paper Parcels

Servings: 6 | Prep Time: 25 Minutes | Cook Time: 15 Minutes

This recipe is not as intimidating as it sounds and the result will make you glad that you tried it.

Ingredients:

4 boneless skinless salmon fillets

1 1/2 teaspoons ginger, grated finely

1 clove garlic, grated finely

1 green onion, chopped finely

1 teaspoon vegetable oil

1/2 teaspoon sea salt flakes

24 rice paper rounds

150 grams enoki mushrooms, trimmed

12 sprigs fresh coriander

2 tablespoons sweet soy sauce, like kecap manis

2 tablespoons rice wine vinegar

1 green onion, sliced thinly

Instructions:

1. Cut filets lengthwise into three pieces.

2. Mix ginger, onion, garlic, oil, and salt in a bowl and mix well.

3. Add salmon to the bowl and toss lightly to coat.

4. Fill a bowl with warm water and set it next to the cutting board.

5. Soak two rice papers in the bowl for about 20 seconds, then lay them on top of each other on the cutting board.

6. Put a sprig of coriander, a few mushrooms, and a piece of salmon in the middle of the rice paper.

7. Fold in the ends of the paper, then roll the parcels shut.

8. Steam for 12 minutes.

9. Combine vinegar and sweet soy sauce; mix well. Serve with salmon packets.

Nutritional Info: Calories: 186 | Sodium: 550 mg | Dietary Fiber: 1.1 g |
Total Fat: 8.2 g | Total Carbs: 3.3 g | Protein: 24.2 g.

Chili Soy Sauce Steamed Fish

Servings: 2 | Prep Time: 5 Minutes | Cook Time 12 Minutes

Fish is super fun to play around with because of all of the different flavors and textures that seafood offers.

Ingredients:

8 ounces whitefish filets (sea bass, cod, halibut, red snapper, or tilapia are all good)

1/2 cup water

3 tablespoons soy sauce

2 tablespoons sesame oil

2 tablespoons thinly sliced ginger

1/3 bok choy, chopped

1 teaspoon chopped cilantro leaves

3 minced garlic cloves

1/2 teaspoon chili powder

1 teaspoon red pepper flakes

1 tablespoon white sugar

Salt and black pepper

Instructions:

1. Season the fish with salt and pepper.

2. Line steamer with parchment paper and gently lay fish over the paper.

3. Gently place bok choy on top of the fish.

4. Steam for 12 minutes.

5. Combine the remaining ingredients in a small sauce pan and bring to a boil.

6. Allow the sauce to simmer and thicken.

7. Put fish and bok choy on serving plates and pour sauce over both, serve immediately.

Nutritional Info: Calories: 329 | Sodium: 2839 mg | Dietary Fiber: 2.5 g | Total Fat: 21.4 g | Total Carbs: 21.7 g | Protein: 4.2 g.

Kristin Amber

Shrimp Shu Mai

Servings: 4 | Prep Time: 40 Minutes | Cook Time: 8 Minutes

This recipe is perfect for any time of day and can make a great entrée or an amazing appetizer.

Ingredients:

9 ounces large shrimp

2 tablespoons egg white (about 1 egg)

1 teaspoon potato starch

1/2 teaspoon salt

1 3/4 ounces pork fat

18 ounces small shelled shrimp

7 ounces calamari steak

4 scallions

3 tablespoons potato starch

1 egg white

1 tablespoon ginger juice

1 tablespoon shaoxing wine

2 teaspoons sugar

2 teaspoons sesame oil

2 teaspoons oyster sauce

1 teaspoon soy sauce

1/2 teaspoon salt

1/4 teaspoon white pepper

32 shumai wrappers

Instructions:

1. Peel the large shrimp and cut them in half lengthwise.
2. Add shrimp, egg white, 1 teaspoon potato starch, and half a teaspoon salt. Mix well until shrimp is coated in white frothy mixture.
3. Peel the small shrimp and put it in a food processor with pork fat and calamari steak.
4. Process until there are no large chunks, but it is not completely smooth.
5. Add Scallions, the rest of the potato starch, wine, egg mix, ginger juice, sesame oil, oyster sauce, soy sauce, salt, and pepper, and pulse to mix.
6. Spray the steamer bowl with non-stick spray
7. To wrap the shumai make an O with your left hand and put the wrapper over the O.
8. Place a heaping teaspoon of the mixture in the center of the O and top with a half large shrimp.
9. Place another teaspoon on top of the shrimp and press it down into the O in your hand.
10. Top with one more half shrimp and gently place in steamer.
11. Repeat until the steamer is full and steam for 8 minutes.

Nutritional Info: Calories: 1335 | Sodium: 3059 mg | Dietary Fiber: 6.3 g |
Total Fat: 24.5 g | Total Carbs: 183.8 g | Protein: 85.2 g.

Spicy Steamed Shrimp

Servings: 2 | Prep Time: 5 Minutes | Cook Time: 20 Minutes

If there is one thing I love more than shrimp it is spice; when you combine the two you get this match made in heaven.

Ingredients:

1 pound tiger prawn shrimp in shells	3 ounces Old Bay seasoning

Instructions:

1. Toss shrimp in seasoning and lay in the steamer bowl.
2. Steam until shrimp turns pink, about 20 minutes.

Nutritional Info: Calories: 269 | Sodium: 11892 mg | Dietary Fiber: 0 g | Total Fat: 3.8 g | Total Carbs: 3.4 g | Protein: 51.7 g.

Steamed Clams and Garlic

Servings: 4 | Prep Time: 20 Minutes | Cook Time: 25 Minutes

This recipe only takes a few ingredients to make a stand out entrée or appetizer.

Ingredients:

50 small clams in shell, scrubbed	1 cup white wine
2 tablespoons extra virgin olive oil	2 tablespoons butter
6 cloves garlic, minced	1/2 cup chopped fresh parsley

Instructions:

1. Wash clams and mince garlic.
2. Place clams in steamer and steam until they just start to open (5-10 minutes)
3. Discard any clams that don't open.
4. Add oil and garlic together in a sauce pan and sauté garlic for one minute.
5. Add wine and boil until wine has been reduced to half.
6. Add butter to the pot and transfer clams to finish cooking. Clams will be finished when they are fully opened.
7. Transfer to a serving bowl and sprinkle with parsley to serve.

Nutritional Info: Calories: 265 | Sodium: 773 mg | Dietary Fiber: 1.1 g | Total Fat: 13.2 g | Total Carbs: 25.5 g | Protein: 1.8 g.

Kristin Amber

Steamed Cod with Warm New Potato and Pea Salad

Servings: 4 | Prep Time: 20 Minutes | Cook Time: 15 Minutes

This is a unique recipe that really stands out on the plate and the palette.

Ingredients:

4 cod fillets, skinned	Olive oil
1 lemon; zest and juice	7 ounces pot crème fraîche
10 ounces new potatoes, scraped and halved if large	1 teaspoon wholegrain mustard
250 grams packet frozen petit pois	Salt and pepper to taste
2 bunches spring onions	

Instructions:

1. Season the fish with salt and pepper, sprinkle with lemon zest and squeeze lemon over fish.

2. Place the filets in the steamer and steam for 12 minutes.

3. While the fish steams, boil the potatoes until cooked through (about 15 minutes).

4. Add peas to the potatoes and let them come back to a boil before removing from heat and draining.

5. Cut onions into 1-inch pieces and fry them in oil for about 3 minutes.

6. Combine crème fraiche, mustard, and a little oil together, then add a little lemon zest and lemon juice.

7. Pour fried onions and crème mix into the potatoes and stir until the potatoes and peas are covered.

8. Dish potato and pea mix onto a plate and lay fish over it to serve.

Nutritional Info: Calories: 429 | Sodium: 234 mg | Dietary Fiber: 5.6 g |
Total Fat: 12.8 g | Total Carbs: 24.5 g | Protein: 52.4 g.

Ginger-Soy Steamed Fish

This Asian inspired recipe is awesome for so many reasons. It tastes great, it only takes 15 minutes to make, and it is healthy to boot.

Ingredients:

- 1 1/2 to 2 pounds white fish fillets
- 6 tablespoons soy sauce
- 2 tablespoons toasted asian sesame oil
- 2 tablespoons asian rice cooking wine
- 4 tablespoons fresh ginger
- 2 teaspoons granulated sugar
- 1 teaspoon garlic powder
- 1/2 teaspoon white pepper
- 1/4 cup freshly chopped cilantro leaves
- 4 stalks thinly sliced green onions

Instructions:

1. Thinly slice your ginger into matchstick sizes slices.
2. Place the fish on a steamer safe plate.
3. Combine all other ingredients, minus the cilantro and onions, together and drizzle over fish.
4. Steam for 12 minutes.
5. Sprinkle cilantro and onions over fish and serve.

Nutritional Info: Calories: 336 | Sodium: 1004 mg | Dietary Fiber: 1.0 g | Total Fat: 16.1 g | Total Carbs: 6.4 g | Protein: 38.6 g.

Kristin Amber

Steamed Fish with Ginger and Orange

Servings: 2 | Prep Time: 5 Minutes | Cook Time: 7 Minutes

If you are worried about steaming fish for the first time, I would suggest this easy, yet flavorful, recipe.

Ingredients:

Olive oil

2 fillets sea bass or bream

2 slices ginger root, finely shredded

1 garlic clove, sliced

1 orange, zested and juiced

Coriander

Instructions:

1. Lightly brush a piece of parchment paper large enough for both fillets.
2. Lay the fillets skin side down on the paper.
3. Sprinkle remaining ingredients over the fish.
4. Steam for 7 minutes. Sprinkle coriander over fish and serve.

Nutritional Info: Calories: 179 | Sodium: 118 mg | Dietary Fiber: 0.8 g | Total Fat: 1.4 g | Total Carbs: 5.1 g | Protein: 34.7 g.

Steamed Garlic and Herb Scallops with Veggies

Servings: 1 | Prep Time: 5 Minutes | Cook Time: 8 Minutes

There are so many benefits to this meal; I don't even know where to begin. It is easy to make, takes a single steamer bowl, and is paleo friendly.

Ingredients:

1 tablespoon oil

1 tablespoon lemon juice

Salt to taste

1/4 teaspoon each dried basil and onion salt

1/4 teaspoon minced garlic

4-5 medium to large scallop

1 cup spinach greens

Instructions:

1. Put scallops in a bowl and add vinegar, toss to coat.
2. Add all other ingredient except spinach and toss again.
3. Put scallops and spinach in the steamer bowl and steam for 8 minutes.
4. Serve immediately.

Nutritional Info: Calories: 264 | Sodium: 548 mg | Dietary Fiber: 0.7 g | Total Fat: 15.0 g | Total Carbs: 5.2 g | Protein: 26.2 g.

Steamed Flounder with Vegetable Couscous

Servings: 4 | Prep Time: 12 Minutes | Cook Time: 12 Minutes

This recipe is not only full of flavor, but incredibly health conscious as well.

Ingredients:

1 cup couscous

1 red bell pepper

1 zucchini

1/2 teaspoon dried oregano

3 tablespoons olive oil

Salt and pepper to taste.

1 tablespoon plus 1 teaspoon Dijon mustard

4 flounder fillets (6 to 8 ounces each)

1 tablespoon white-wine vinegar

Instructions:

1. Divide one tablespoon of mustard and spread evenly over flounder.

2. Steam flounder for 12 minutes.

3. While the flounder steams, dice pepper and zucchini.

4. Combine couscous, zucchini, pepper, oregano, 1 tablespoon oil, and 1 1/4 cups water in a microwave safe bowl.

5. Season with salt and pepper and cover.

6. Microwave on high for 3 minutes, then stir.

7. In a small bowl, mix together teaspoon mustard, vinegar, remaining oil, and salt and pepper to create a vinaigrette.

8. Place fish on couscous, drizzle with vinaigrette, and serve.

Nutritional Info: Calories: 550 | Sodium: 249 mg | Dietary Fiber: 3.8 g |
Total Fat: 15.3 g | Total Carbs: 38.1 g | Protein: 61.9 g.

Kristin Amber

Steamed Ginger and Soy Fish

Servings: 4 | Prep Time: 20 Minutes | Cook Time: 5 Minutes

This is another recipe that will make you look like a gourmet chef without needing to put too much time or effort into it.

Ingredients:

4 (200 grams) ling fillets

1 bunch coriander, leaves picked

4 spring onions, sliced

1 long red chili, thinly sliced

steamed rice, to serve

1/2 cup light soy sauce

2 cloves garlic, shredded

2 tablespoons ginger, shredded

1 stick lemongrass, white part thinly sliced

1/4 cup sweet soy sauce, like kecap manis

1/4 cup brown rice vinegar

1/2 teaspoon sesame oil

Instructions:

1. Pat the fish dry and place in your steamer, steam for 5 minutes.
2. Combine the soy sauce with all other ingredients below it in a small sauce pan.
3. Add 1/2 cup of water and simmer for 5 minutes.
4. Place steamed rice on a plate and lay the fish on top.
5. Pour half of ginger sauce over fish and top with coriander, onion, and chilies.
6. Serve with remaining ginger sauce.

Nutritional Info: Calories: 287 | Sodium: 2859 mg | Dietary Fiber: 1.5 g | Total Fat: 2.6 g | Total Carbs: 12.1 g | Protein: 49.8 g.

Steamed Cod with Crisp Vegetables

Servings: 4 | Prep Time: 10 Minutes | Cook Time: 15 Minutes

Cod is a fish with a unique taste that you can do a lot with. This recipe is a simple one, but it is still amazingly flavorful.

Ingredients:

16 thin asparagus, halved crosswise

1/4 pound snow peas

1 small zucchini, quartered lengthwise and sliced 1/4-inch-thick

1 small red bell pepper, thinly sliced

1/2 cup chopped mixed herbs, such as tarragon, chives and parsley

Salt and pepper to taste

4 (6-ounce) cod fillets

1/4 cup dry white wine

2 tablespoons unsalted butter

Instructions:

1. Lay out four separate pieces of foil out and pile equal amounts of vegetables on each piece of foil.

2. Sprinkle herbs over the veggies and season with salt and pepper.

3. Add cod to the top of the veggies and season with salt and pepper.

4. Add a tablespoon of wine and a 1/2 tablespoon of butter to the top of each filet.

5. Fold the edges of the foil around the fish and veggies to create a packet.

6. Steam for 15 minutes.

7. Allow foil to cool then remove from packets and serve.

Nutritional Info: Calories: 289 | Sodium: 182 mg | Dietary Fiber: 4.7 g |
Total Fat: 7.7 g | Total Carbs: 9.8 g | Protein: 42.5 g.

Kristin Amber

Steamed Lobster Tail

Servings: 4 | Prep Time: Thawing | Cook Time: 6 Minutes

Lobster tail is the epitome of decadence, and another way to prove that your steamer can cook the most delicious foods you can find.

Ingredients:

4 1/4 pounds thawed lobster tails
melted butter

Instructions:

1. Place tails in the steamer with room in between each.

2. Steam for 6 minutes.

3. Serve hot with melted butter or your choice of sauce.

Nutritional Info: Calories: 440 | Sodium: 2349 mg | Dietary Fiber: 0 g | Total Fat: 5.0 g | Total Carbs: 0 g | Protein: 91.6 g.

Steamed Snow Crab Legs

Servings: 2 | Prep Time: Time to Thaw | Cook Time: 8 Minutes

This is recipe could seriously not get any simpler, but it is a reminder that your steamer can cook just about anything.

Ingredients:

4 snow crab legs

Instructions:

1. Thaw and rinse the crab legs.

2. Place crabs in the steamer bowl and steam for 8 minutes.

3. Serve while still hot.

Nutritional Info: Calories: 260 | Sodium: 2230 mg | Dietary Fiber: 0 g | Total Fat: 4.1 g | Total Carbs: 0 g | Protein: 51.9 g.

Steamed Mahi Mahi

Servings: 4 | Prep Time: 10 Minutes | Cook Time: 20 Minutes

Mahi Mahi is not just a great tasting fish, but it is also fun to say.

Ingredients:

1 1/4 cups white rice

3 scallions, thinly sliced (white and green parts separated)

2 tablespoons minced peeled ginger

1 1/2 pounds skinless center-cut mahi mahi fillet (1 1/2 inches thick)

1/4 teaspoon ground white pepper, plus more to taste

4 heads baby bok choy, halved lengthwise

2 carrots, sliced 1/4-inch-thick

3 tablespoons vegetable oil

1 fresno or red jalapeno chili pepper, sliced (remove seeds for less heat)

2 cloves garlic, minced

Salt

2 tablespoons low-sodium soy sauce

Instructions:

1. Cook rice per instructions on bag.
2. Sprinkle scallion whites and a teaspoon of ginger on a steamer safe plate.
3. Lay fish over scallions and ginger and season with 1/4 teaspoon white pepper.
4. Place the fish in the steamer and steam for 8 minutes.
5. Add bok choy and carrots to the second tier and steam at the same time as your fish.
6. While the fish and veggies steam, heat the vegetable oil in a skillet and add garlic, the rest of the ginger, chili, and 1/2 teaspoon salt. Mix and cook for about 3 minutes.
7. Remove the fish from the basket and continue to steam the vegetables until soft.
8. Remove any excess liquids from the plate and quarter the fish.
9. Put the fish and vegetables on 4 separate plates and drizzle with chili sauce and soy sauce.
10. Top with scallion greens and white pepper and serve.

Nutritional Info: Calories: 595 | Sodium: 1242 mg | Dietary Fiber: 10.8 g |
Total Fat: 14.0 g | Total Carbs: 71.7 g | Protein: 50.2 g.

Steamed Salmon with Snow Peas

Servings: 2 | Prep Time: 10 Minutes | Cook Time: 12 Minutes

Salmon is a great fish because it has a unique flavor, is sustainable, and can be prepared in numerous ways.

Ingredients:

1 1/2 teaspoons fresh lime juice

1 teaspoon soy sauce

1 scallion

1/2 teaspoon toasted sesame oil

1/2 teaspoon grated fresh ginger

1/2 teaspoon minced garlic

2 salmon fillets, skin removed, about 1 1/2-inch-thick

Nonstick cooking spray

1/2 pound snow peas

Instructions:

1. Thinly slice scallion with whites and two inches of greens.
2. Add scallions in a bowl with oil and lime juice, mix well and set aside.
3. Mince garlic and grate ginger, then rub them on the salmon.
4. Coat the steamer bowl with cooking spray and lay the salmon down gently in the bowl.
5. Place snow peas in second bowl and steam both for 12 minutes.
6. Put snow peas on two separate plates and top with fish.
7. Drizzle with lime sauce and serve.

Nutritional Info: Calories: 300 | Sodium: 234 mg | Dietary Fiber: 3.5 g | Total Fat: 12.4 g | Total Carbs: 9.6 g | Protein: 38.6 g.

Steamed Scallops with Soy Sauce and Garlic Oil

Servings: 3 – 4 | Prep Time: 5 Minutes | Cook Time: 5 Minutes

Scallops do not get the credit they deserve as one of the tastier mollusks.

Ingredients:

6-8 scallops on the half shell

1 stalk scallion

3 teaspoons low sodium soy sauce

1 teaspoon sugar

1 teaspoon water

3 cloves garlic

2 tablespoon oil

Instructions:

1. Mix the soy sauce, sugar, and water well and set aside.

2. Cut scallions diagonally and finely chop the garlic.

3. Heat oil in a pan and add garlic, sautéing for about 3 minutes.

4. Place scallops on a steamer safe plate and pour soy mix over the scallops.

5. Steam for 5 minutes or until scallops start to turn opaque.

6. Drizzle garlic oil over the scallops and top with scallions to serve.

Nutritional Info: Calories: 124 | Sodium: 231 mg | Dietary Fiber: 0 g | Total Fat: 7.3 g | Total Carbs: 4.0 g | Protein: 10.5 g.

Kristin Amber

Steamed Scallion Ginger Fish Fillets with Bok Choy

Servings: 4 | Prep Time: 20 Minutes | Cook Time: 15 Minutes

I love recipes like this one because they taste great, are easy to make, and make you look like you are a gourmet cook fresh out of France.

Ingredients:

1/2 cup light soy sauce

2 tablespoons sugar

1/2 cup rice wine

1/2 teaspoon five-spice powder

2 pounds sole fillet, cut into 8 pieces

1 (1-inch) piece fresh ginger, finely julienned

6 tablespoons vegetable oil

8 scallions (white and green parts), cut crosswise into 2-inch lengths, then thinly julienned lengthwise

Stir-fried baby bok choy

Instructions:

1. Mix the first 4 ingredients together in a medium bowl.

2. Place fish on a rimmed dish and drizzle with a tablespoon of soy sauce mixture.

3. Sprinkle scallions over the fish, cover and refrigerate for 15 minutes.

4. Transfer plate to the steamer and steam for 12 minutes.

5. Add bok choy into second tier bowl and steam at the same time as the fish.

6. While the fish and bok choy steam, heat the oil over medium heat.

7. Divide the fish onto four plates and top with scallions, pour a little oil over each filet and serve with bok choy.

Nutritional Info: Calories: 553 | Sodium: 2301 mg | Dietary Fiber: 1.4 g | Total Fat: 24.1 g | Total Carbs: 26.1 g | Protein: 57.6 g.

x

Steamed White Fish with Shiitake-Seaweed Broth

Servings: 4 | Prep Time: 1 Hour 30 Minutes | Cook Time: 15 Minutes

This is actually a very flavorful dish that plays around on the palate and never really locks down a single flavor.

Ingredients:

Broth:

1 tablespoon bacon fat or canola oil	3 cloves garlic, peeled
1 tablespoon. sesame oil	1 teaspoon Sichuan peppercorns
1/2 cup cilantro stems	1 1/2 ounces dried shiitake mushrooms
4 scallions, chopped into 3-inch pieces	10 sheets dried seaweed
1/4 red onion, chopped	1/4–1/3 cup soy sauce
1 lemongrass root, minced	Salt to taste

Fish:

4 (5-ounce) pieces white fish, preferably cod or halibut	1/2 cup ponzu sauce
1 lemongrass root, minced	2 tablespoons sesame oil
1 clove garlic, minced	Salt and pepper to taste
	Sliced scallions, for garnish

Instructions:

1. Combine bacon fat and sesame oil in a large skillet over medium heat.
2. Add cilantro stems, scallions, onions, garlic, peppercorn, and lemon grass. Sauté the mixture for about a minute.
3. Add 5 cups of water to the mixture and bring to a boil.
4. Reduce to a simmer and add szeaweed and mushrooms, continue to simmer for 35 minutes.
5. While the sauce simmers, place the fish into a shallow dish and sprinkle with lemon grass and garlic.
6. Season with salt and pepper and drizzle ponzu sauce and sesame over the fish.
7. Cover with foil and marinate in the refrigerator for 30 minutes.
8. Strain the broth into a bowl through a mess strainer, then add soy sauce and salt to taste.
9. Remove the fish from the marinade and brush off extra lemongrass and garlic.
10. Steam for 15 minutes.
11. Pour broth on a plate and add fish, top with scallions and serve.

Nutritional Info: Calories: 5804 | Sodium: 4711 mg | Dietary Fiber: 1.2 g |
Total Fat: 132.6 g | Total Carbs: 10.1 g | Protein: 1074.3 g.

Kristin Amber

Thai Steamed Fish with Lime, Garlic & Chilies

Servings: 2 | Prep Time: 10 Minutes | Cook Time: 15 Minutes

This Asian inspired recipe hits all the right notes and is surprisingly simple to make. It is a great recipe to fool guests into thinking you are a 5-star chef.

Ingredients

1 1/2 pounds skinless fish fillets	Juice of one large lime
2 tablespoons fish sauce	3 large garlic cloves
1 teaspoon sugar	5-6 chilies
1 teaspoon chicken bouillon granules	A handful of fresh cilantro leaves

Instructions:

1. Place the fish on a steamer safe plate.
2. Chop the garlic and chilies thinly, but don't mince them as they will release too many oils and overwhelm the fish.
3. Sprinkle the garlic and chilies over the fish evenly.
4. Set aside the cilantro and mix all other ingredients together.
5. Pour over fish and steam for 15 minutes.
6. Sprinkle cilantro over fish and serve.

Nutritional Info: Calories: 833 | Sodium: 3220 mg | Dietary Fiber: 3.0 g | Total Fat: 42.1 g | Total Carbs: 67.7 g | Protein: 51.8 g.

Whole Steamed Fish

Servings: 1 | Prep Time: 20 Minutes | Cook Time: 15 Minutes

This recipe may make some people uneasy, but if you are daring enough to try it, there is a good chance that you will like it.

Ingredients:

1 whole striped bass or sea bass (about 1 1/2 pounds), cleaned

3 tablespoons fresh ginger

2 scallions

8 sprigs fresh cilantro

1/4 cup plus 2 tablespoons canola oil

1/4 cup water

1/4 teaspoon salt

1/4 cup light soy sauce

White pepper to taste

Instructions:

1. Julienne ginger and scallions (both white and green parts) and chop cilantro.

2. Remove any scales from your fish using a filet or steak knife.

3. Cut of fins, but leave the head and tail intact.

4. Looking in the cavity, you should see the backbone. It is also possible that you will see a membrane that you should pierce and cut, revealing a blood line near the bone. Run your finger or a spoon across it to clean it thoroughly.

5. Remove the gills if there are any left.

6. Rinse the fish off and transfer it to a steamer safe plate.

7. Steam for 9 Minutes.

8. Remove any excess fluid from the plate and top the fish with half of the ginger, the green portion of the scallions, and cilantro.

9. Heat two tablespoons of oil in a small sauce pan and add the other half of the ginger, cook until it begins to sizzle.

10. Add water, soy sauce, salt, and pepper to the ginger and cook until simmering.

11. Add the white portion of the scallions along with the rest of the oil and continue cooking until simmering.

12. Once it is ready pour the ginger mixture over the fish and serve.

Nutritional Info: Calories: 195 | Sodium: 106 mg | Dietary Fiber: 3.3 g |
Total Fat: 3.7 g | Total Carbs: 14.3 g | Protein: 26.3 g.

Kristin Amber

CHAPTER

6

Pork and Beef

Cantonese Steamed Pork

Servings: 4 | Prep Time: 25 Minutes | Cook Time: 12 Minutes

This Asian inspired recipe takes a boring Sunday night meal and makes it something to not only be remembered, but craved.

Ingredients:

1 1/2 cups long-grain white rice

1/2 cup fat-skimmed beef broth

About 2 tablespoons reduced-sodium soy sauce

1 tablespoon dry sherry

1 tablespoon minced fresh ginger

1 large clove garlic, minced

2 teaspoons firmly packed brown sugar

1/4 teaspoon hot chili flakes

1 pound pork tenderloin, cut into 1/2-inch crosswise slices

About 1 1/3 pounds baby bok choy

Instructions:

1. Cook rice as per the instructions on the bag.
2. In a shallow bowl, combine brown sugar, sherry, beef broth, 2 tablespoon soy sauce, ginger, garlic, and chili flakes.
3. Turn pork over in the mixture, then cover and refrigerate for 15 minutes.
4. Place pork in the bottom steamer bowl and bok choy on the top.
5. Steam for 12 minutes and serve hot with rice.
6. If you want, you can reheat the broth mix and pour over the rice for extra flavor.

Nutritional Info: Calories: 460 | Sodium: 714 mg | Dietary Fiber: 2.7 g |
Total Fat: 5.0 g | Total Carbs: 62.2 g | Protein: 38.2 g.

Chinese Steamed Pork Balls

Servings: 6 | Prep Time: 30 Minutes | Cook Time: 30 Minutes

I love recipes like this one because, not only is it delicious, but it just goes to show how versatile a food steamer can be.

Ingredients:

3/4 pounds pork, ground	1 1/2 teaspoons rice wine
1/2 teaspoons fresh ginger, minced	1 teaspoon sugar
3 spring onions, chopped	2 tablespoons light soy sauce
5 water chestnut, finely chopped	1 teaspoon dark soy sauce
4 dried shiitake mushrooms	1/2 teaspoon salt
2 teaspoon cornstarch	1 1/2 tablespoon canola oil

Instructions:

1. Soak the mushroom for about 20 minutes, then drain them and chop them.

2. In a large bowl, combine all ingredients until mixed thoroughly.

3. Form the mixture into balls about an inch in diameter.

4. Place in your steamer with space in between each ball and steam for 20 minutes.

5. The meat will brown so you know that they are done.

Nutritional Info: Calories: 188 | Sodium: 707 mg | Dietary Fiber: 1.3 g | Total Fat: 5.7 g | Total Carbs: 18.0 g | Protein: 16.6 g.

Pork Dumplings

Servings: 18 – 20 | Prep Time: 30 Minutes | Cook Time: 10 Minutes

This recipe is a guaranteed hit as an appetizer or snack and will be the talk of your next potluck or get together.

Ingredients:

1 pound ground pork

1 cup thinly sliced napa cabbage

1/2 cup chopped scallions (both white and green parts)

1/4 cup chopped fresh cilantro

1 1/2 tablespoons soy sauce

1 tablespoon finely chopped garlic

1 tablespoon rice vinegar

1 tablespoon cornstarch

2 teaspoons finely chopped fresh ginger

1 1/2 teaspoons asian sesame oil

1 teaspoon granulated sugar

1/2 teaspoon black pepper

1 large egg white

55 to 60 siomai wrappers or wonton wrappers

Instructions:

1. Combine all ingredients (other than wrappers) and mix until even throughout.

2. Remove the wonton wrappers from the package and cover with a damp cloth.

3. One at a time, brush the edges of the wrapper with water and spoon 1 teaspoon of the pork mix into the center.

4. Close the wrapper and set on a baking sheet, cover with a damp cloth.

5. Repeat until all your wrappers are filled.

6. Spray the bottom of your steamer bowl with vegetable spray.

7. Place as many wrappers as you can in the bowl with a little space between each one.

8. Steam for 10 minutes and serve immediately.

Nutritional Info: Calories: 322 | Sodium: 612 mg | Dietary Fiber: 1.9 g |
Total Fat: 2.6 g | Total Carbs: 56.8 g | Protein: 15.7 g.

Shomai

There are many ways to prepare dumplings and all of them offer their own unique flavor profiles.

Ingredients:

- 2 pounds boneless country style pork ribs
- 4 scallions, minced
- 3 cloves garlic, minced
- 1 1/2 teaspoons fresh ginger, grated
- 3 teaspoons salt
- 1/2 teaspoon pepper, or more to taste
- 2 teaspoons Shaoxing wine
- 2 teaspoons soy sauce
- 2 egg whites, lightly beaten
- 60-80 wonton wrappers

Instructions:

1. Cut ribs into 1/4-inch cubes and spread over a baking sheet.
2. Cover with plastic wrap and freeze for 30 minutes.
3. Place half of the pork into a food processor and process until the pork is small chunks, but not a paste.
4. Transfer to a medium bowl, then repeat with the other half of the pork.
5. Add all other ingredients other than the wrappers to the pork and mix well, you may even want to combine with your hands.
6. Remove the wonton wrappers from the package and cover with a damp cloth.
7. One at a time, brush the edges of the wrapper with water and spoon 1 teaspoon of the pork mix into the center.
8. Close the wrapper and set on a baking sheet, cover with a damp cloth.
9. Repeat until all your wrappers are filled.
10. Spray the bottom of your steamer bowl with vegetable spray.
11. Place as many wrappers as you can in the bowl with a little space between each one.
12. Steam for 10 minutes and serve immediately or place in the oven on low to keep warm since it will take multiple batches.

Nutritional Info: Calories: 408 | Sodium: 958 mg | Dietary Fiber: 1.9 g |
Total Fat: 9.5 g | Total Carbs: 56.1 g | Protein: 21.9 g.

Kristin Amber

Fragrant Citrus Steamed Pork

Servings: 2 | Prep Time: 10 Minutes | Cook Time: 25 Minutes

This recipe is bursting with flavor as well as being a unique flavor combination.

Ingredients:

2 boneless pork chops

2 tablespoons fresh orange juice

2 cups water

1/4 teaspoon ground cloves

1/4 teaspoon ground coriander

1/4 teaspoon ground cinnamon

1 pinch cayenne pepper, or to taste

Instructions:

1. In a small sauce pan, bring water, orange juice, and spices to a soft boil.

2. Add mixture to your steamer and lay pork chops in the bowl.

3. Steam for 23 minutes, serve immediately.

Nutritional Info: Calories: 152 | Sodium: 65 mg | Dietary Fiber: 0 g | Total Fat: 3.6 g | Total Carbs: 2.1 g | Protein: 26.3 g.

Steamed BBQ Pork Buns

Servings: 10 | Prep Time: 3 Hours | Cook Time: 30 Minutes

This is an entire meal (or appetizer) all in one, and is sure to be a crowd pleaser.

Ingredients:

1 teaspoon active dry yeast

3/4 cups warm water

2 cups all-purpose flour

1 cup cornstarch

5 tablespoons sugar

1/4 cup canola or vegetable oil

2 1/2 teaspoons baking powder

1 tablespoon olive oil

1/3 cup finely chopped shallots or red onion

1 tablespoon sugar

1 tablespoon light soy sauce

1 1/2 tablespoons oyster sauce

1 tablespoon sesame oil

2 teaspoons dark soy sauce

1/2 cup chicken stock

2 tablespoons flour

1 1/2 cups diced Chinese roast pork

Instructions:

1. Dissolve the yeast in warm water.

2. Sift together flour and corn starch.

3. Combine yeast mix, flour mix, sugar, and olive oil.

4. Knead until it forms a smooth dough, then cover and let sit for two hours.

5. Heat the oil over medium heat and add onion, sautéing for 1 minute.

6. Add sugar, soy sauce, oyster sauce, sesame oil, and soy sauces, stir until the mixture begins to bubble.

7. Add chicken sauce and flour, continue to stir until the sauce thickens.

8. Stir in the roast pork and remove from heat.

9. Add baking powder to the dough and knead until smooth again, cover for 15 minutes.

10. Cut parchment paper into 4 x 4 inch squares.

11. Roll the dough into a thick log and cut into 10 equal pieces.

12. Roll the pieces into balls and then flatten them into circles.

13. Spoon equal parts of the pork mix into the center of each circle.

14. Fold the circle up and around the mixture, pinch together to seal.

15. Set the buns on parchment paper steam side down and add to the steamer.

16. Steam for 12 minutes.

Nutritional Info: Calories: 302 | Sodium: 272 mg | Dietary Fiber: 1.1 g |
Total Fat: 9.8 g | Total Carbs: 40.7 g | Protein: 12.4 g.

Kristin Amber

Steamed Cheeseburgers

Servings: 4 | Prep Time: 10 Minutes | Cook Time: 12 Minutes

Everyone love a good cheeseburger; this recipe is proof that you can cook anything in a steamer.

Ingredients:

1 1/2 pounds 85 percent lean ground beef

2 teaspoons soy sauce

1 teaspoon onion powder

1 teaspoon tomato paste

3/4 teaspoons salt

3/4 teaspoons pepper

4 ounces sharp cheddar cheese, shredded (1 cup)

4 hamburger buns

Instructions:

1. In a medium bowl, combine beef, soy sauce, tomato paste, onion powder, salt, and pepper.

2. Separate into 4 equal portions and roll into balls.

3. Flatten the balls into patties and press a small divot into the center of each patty.

4. Place the patties in the steamer and steam for 12 minutes.

5. Remove steamer lid and evenly divide cheese among patties, replace the lid and allow the cheese to melt.

6. Place the bun tops on top of the burgers and the bun bottoms on the bottom of bun tops to warm (about 30 seconds.)

7. Remove and assemble to serve.

Nutritional Info: Calories: 556 | Sodium: 1083 mg | Dietary Fiber: 1.1 g |
Total Fat: 21.9 g | Total Carbs: 22.8 g | Protein: 63.1 g.

Stuffed Steamed Bitter Gourd

When you pull this one off, people will not believe that you are not a professional cook.

Ingredients:

1 bitter gourd, medium-sized

1 teaspoon salt

300 – 350 grams minced pork

1 yellow onion, finely chopped

1 stalk spring onion, finely chopped

1 clove garlic, finely chopped

1 teaspoon grated ginger

1 tablespoon oyster sauce

1/2 tablespoon light soy sauce

1 teaspoon sugar

1/2 teaspoon pepper

2 teaspoons sesame oil

1 tablespoon corn starch

Instructions:

1. Cut the gourd into 1/2-inch slices and scrape out the seeds.

2. Rub salt into the slices and let sit in a bowl for 15 minutes.

3. Drain and rinse the slices, then set aside.

4. Combine minced pork, onion, spring onion, garlic, ginger, and seasonings in a medium bowl and mix until ingredients are even throughout.

5. Stuff each slice with the pork mixture and place on a steamer safe plate. Steam for 30 minutes.

Nutritional Info: Calories: 192 | Sodium: 776 mg | Dietary Fiber: 0.8 g |
Total Fat: 5.4 g | Total Carbs: 11.2 g | Protein: 24.3 g.

Kristin Amber

Steamed Minced Pork with Water Chestnut

Servings: 4 | Prep Time: 15 Minutes | Cook Time: 12 Minutes

This is a unique recipe that you won't come across every day. It is another example of how your steamer can cook gourmet meals.

Ingredients:

3/4 pounds lean minced pork

2 water chestnuts, peeled, minced finely

2 shallots, peeled, minced finely

1 clove garlic, peeled, minced finely

5-inch length ginger, peeled, minced finely

1 stalk spring onion, finely chopped

2 tablespoons salted radish, minced finely

1 egg yolk

1 tablespoon light soy sauce

1 teaspoon sesame oil

1 tablespoon corn flour

1/2 teaspoon ground white pepper

Dash salt

2 tablespoons shallot oil

Instructions:

1. In a large bowl, combine pork, light soy sauce, sesame oil, corn flour, salt, and pepper.
2. Mix together, even kneading with your hands if necessary.
3. Add the egg yolk and continue to mix until the mixture becomes a paste.
4. Pour a 1/2 tablespoon of shallot oil over a small steamer safe plate.
5. Spoon half of the pork mixture onto the plate and flatten with the back side of the spoon to form a patty.
6. Drizzle another 1/2 tablespoon of shallot oil over the patty.
7. Repeat in a second dish and place both dishes in the steamer.
8. Steam for 12 minutes, check for doneness, and serve.

Nutritional Info: Calories: 310 | Sodium: 227 mg | Dietary Fiber: 0.8 g | Total Fat: 17.8 g | Total Carbs: 11.1 g | Protein: 26.1 g.

Steamed Pork Ribs in Black Bean Sauce

Servings: 4 | Prep Time: 2 Hours 30 Minutes | Cook Time: 30 Minutes

You know that pork ribs are delicious, but did you know you could cook them in a steamer?

Ingredients:

400 g pork ribs, chopped into small pieces

1/2 teaspoon bicarbonate of soda

Spring onions

1 tablespoon fermented black beans – rinsed, drained and leave whole or you can mash gently with back of spoon

1 tablespoon finely chopped garlic

1 tablespoon light soy sauce

1 1/2 tablespoon corn flour

2 teaspoons Shaoxing wine

1 teaspoon sesame oil

1 teaspoon sugar

1/4 teaspoon salt

White Rice

Instructions:

1. Cook white rice per instructions on the bag.

2. Wash and drain the spare ribs.

3. Toss in bicarbonate of soda and set aside for 1 hour to allow to tenderize.

4. Wash off soda and pat dry with paper towels.

5. Combine all other ingredients (minus spring onions) in a bowl to create a marinade.

6. Marinate ribs for at least an hour.

7. Place ribs on a steamer safe plate and place it in the steamer.

8. Steam for 25 minutes, garnish with spring onions and serve over rice.

Nutritional Info: Calories: 341 | Sodium: 591 mg | Dietary Fiber: 1.3 g | Total Fat: 19.3 g | Total Carbs: 11.7 g | Protein: 28.2 g.

CHAPTER

7

Poultry

Asian Chicken Parcels

Servings: 4 | Prep Time: 15 Minutes | Cook Time: 10 Minutes

This is an incredibly unique dish that you will not find anywhere else.

Ingredients:

1 medium savoy or Chinese cabbage

2 cloves garlic, peeled

1-inch piece fresh ginger, peeled

6 scallions, white and light green parts, roughly chopped

1/4 cup fresh cilantro leaves

1 to 2 fresh small red chili peppers

1 tablespoon fish sauce

4 trimmed boneless skinless chicken thighs, roughly chopped (about 1 pound)

1 (8-ounce) can water chestnuts

2 tablespoons juice and 2 teaspoons grated zest from 2 limes

1 teaspoon sesame oil

Instructions:

1. Add some salt to a large pot of water and boil.

2. Remove outer leaves of cabbage and cut off stem, separate leaves.

3. Plunge the leaves into the boiling water and blanch for about 2 minutes.

4. Move leaves to a bowl of cold water to cool.

5. Drain the leaves and set them aside.

6. Combine garlic, ginger, scallions, cilantro, red chilies, fish sauce, and a 1/4 teaspoon of salt into a food processor and process until minced.

7. Add the chicken, water chestnuts, lime zest and juice, and sesame oil to the processor and pulse until you create a paste.

8. Lay out the leaves and place about 2 tablespoons of mixture at the lower middle part of the leaf.

9. Fold over edges of the leaves and roll to create a packet.

10. Steam for 8 Minutes and serve.

Nutritional Info: Calories: 356 | Sodium: 534 mg | Dietary Fiber: 3.1 g |
Total Fat: 10.4 g | Total Carbs: 28.5 g | Protein: 37.1 g.

Simple Steamed Chicken and Asparagus

Servings: 2 | Prep Time: 5 Minutes | Cook Time: 15 Minutes

This recipe is great for a few reasons, the main two being that it is super simple and low in calories.

Ingredients:

2 large boneless skinless chicken breast halves

18 ounces of fresh asparagus

Salt and pepper to taste

Instructions:

1. Trim the asparagus, cutting off the rough stalks.

2. Rinse the chicken then season with salt and pepper.

3. Place the chicken and asparagus next to each other in the same bowl and steam for 15 minutes.

Nutritional Info: Calories: 289 | Sodium: 113 mg | Dietary Fiber: 5.4 g |
Total Fat: 9.6 g | Total Carbs: 9.9 g | Protein: 41.8 g.

Kristin Amber

Chicken Legs Steamed with Thyme

Servings: 4 | Prep Time: 30 Minutes | Cook Time: 30 Minutes

This is an amazing recipe that is simple and delicious.

Ingredients:

2 tablespoons olive oil

1 small onion, minced

2 ounces button mushrooms, quartered

8 ounces skinless, boneless chicken breast, chopped

salt and freshly ground black pepper

1/4 cup port wine

1/2 cup chicken stock

2 tablespoons chopped parsley leaves

4 chicken legs with thighs

1-quart chicken broth or stock

3 or 4 fresh thyme sprigs

2 tablespoons extra-virgin olive oil

Instructions:

1. Heat oil in a medium skillet and add onions, sauté for a minute.

2. Add mushrooms and chicken breast and cook until chicken begins to brown.

3. Remove from heat and add salt, pepper, and port.

4. Return to heat and cook until the wine is reduced by a quarter, then add chicken stock and cook for another 2 minutes.

5. Remove the chicken and mushrooms from the pan using a slotted spoon and place it in a bowl.

6. Increase the heat of the left-over liquid and heat until it thickens.

7. Add the liquid and parsley to the bowl and mix the ingredients well.

8. Remove the bone from each of your chicken legs.

9. Lay the legs skin side down and pour the mixture into each bone cavity.

10. Close the cavity and pin closed with a tooth pick.

11. Add thyme to your water and lay the legs flat in the steamer bowl.

12. Steam for 25 minutes and serve.

Nutritional Info: Calories: 436 | Sodium: 983 mg | Dietary Fiber: 2.0 g |
Total Fat: 27.1 g | Total Carbs: 7.6 g | Protein: 40.8 g.

Lemon and Thyme Steamed Chicken

Servings: 4 | Prep Time: 10 Minutes | Cook Time: 15 Minutes

The lemon and thyme complement each other nicely to bring out a host of flavors.

Ingredients:

2 lemons

1 bunch thyme

4 chicken breasts (sliced in half horizontally)

6 cloves garlic (peeled)

2 bunches broccolini (trimmed)

2 small courgettes (sliced thickly)

1 cup natural yoghurt

1 tablespoon honey

1 teaspoon Dijon mustard

Salt and pepper to taste

Instructions:

1. Slice lemons thinly and lay half at the bottom of the steamer basket.

2. Sprinkle half the thyme over lemon slices.

3. Add chicken to the steamer and season with salt and pepper.

4. Top with garlic and other half of lemons and thyme.

5. Add veggies to the second bowl and place on top of first bowl.

6. Steam for 15 minutes.

7. While the chicken steams mix together yogurt, honey, and mustard to create a sauce to serve with the chicken.

Nutritional Info: Calories: 396 | Sodium: 195 mg | Dietary Fiber: 5.9 g |
Total Fat: 13.8 g | Total Carbs: 22.3 g | Protein: 47.9 g.

Kristin Amber

Steamed Soy Marinated Chicken

Servings: 4 | Prep Time: 35 minutes | Cook Time: 15 Minutes

Many recipes call for soy sauce, but not many of them really allow soy to shine like this one does.

Ingredients:

1 cup low-sodium soy sauce	1 cloves garlic, sliced
1 tablespoon sesame oil	1 handful cilantro, chopped
1 tablespoon peanut oil	4 boneless, skinless chicken breasts
1/2 lime, juiced	1 head savoy cabbage
1 (1-inch) piece ginger, sliced thick	

Instructions:

1. Combine soy sauce, sesame oil, peanut oil, lime juice, ginger, garlic, and cilantro in a large sealable bag.
2. Seal the bag and shake to mix well.
3. Add the chicken breast to the bag, seal, and refrigerate for at least 30 minutes.
4. Remove leaves from cabbage and line the bottom of the steamer bowl.
5. Place chicken on cabbage leaves and steam for 15 minutes.

Nutritional Info: Calories: 385 | Sodium: 3736 mg | Dietary Fiber: 5.5 g |
Total Fat: 16.4 g | Total Carbs: 17.4 g | Protein: 42.8 g.

Sesame Chicken Pot Stickers

Servings: 12 | Prep Time: 10 Minutes | Cook Time: 10 Minutes

Pot stickers are always a hit when it comes to an appetizer. These sesame chicken pot stickers add some flair to an already great dish.

Ingredients:

1 pound ground chicken

3 ounces shiitake mushrooms, diced

2 cloves garlic, pressed

2 green onions, thinly sliced

2 tablespoons reduced sodium soy sauce

1 tablespoon sesame oil

1 tablespoon freshly grated ginger

1 teaspoon rice vinegar

1/4 teaspoon white pepper

36 wonton wrappers

Instructions:

1. Combine all ingredients except for wrappers into a bowl and mix together until even.

2. Remove the wonton wrappers from the package and cover with a damp cloth.

3. One at a time, brush the edges of the wrapper with water and spoon a little chicken mix into the center.

4. Fold the wrapper in half and press closed with a fork all the way around the edge.

5. Set on a baking sheet, cover with a damp cloth. Repeat until all your wrappers are filled.

6. Add to steamer and steam for 10 minutes.

Nutritional Info: Calories: 370 | Sodium: 750 mg | Dietary Fiber: 2.0 g | Total Fat: 5.4 g | Total Carbs: 57.5 g | Protein: 20.8 g.

Simple Chinese Steamed Chicken

Servings: 4 | Prep Time: 30 Minutes | Cook Time: 30 Minutes

It is all in the name, this is a simple yet flavorful recipe that can be thrown together in a matter of minutes with very little active time.

Ingredients:

1/2 whole chicken

1/2 teaspoon salt

1 tablespoon garlic, minced

1 tablespoon ginger, minced

1 tablespoon soy sauce

1 1/2 tablespoons olive oil

1 tablespoon chopped green onions

Instructions:

1. Rinse the chicken and pat it dry with paper towels.

2. Rub salt evenly over the chicken and set it aside for 30 minutes.

3. Place the chicken in the steamer and steam for 30 minutes.

4. Cut the chicken into chunks and set aside.

5. Place the oil in a pan over medium heat and add garlic, sauté for 3 minutes.

6. Add ginger and sauté for another 3 minutes.

7. Transfer to a small bowl and mix with soy sauce.

8. Pour soy mixture over the chicken and top with green onions to serve.

Nutritional Info: Calories: 174 | Sodium: 571 mg | Dietary Fiber: 0 g | Total Fat: 10.0 g | Total Carbs: 2.1 g | Protein: 18.6 g.

Steamed Chicken Rice Balls

Servings: 6 | Prep Time: 4 Hours | Cook Time: 30 Minutes

This one takes some planning, but the result is worth the preparation.

Ingredients:

1 cup uncooked short-grain white rice

1 pound ground chicken

1 egg, well beaten

3/4 cups finely chopped onion

1 can (8 ounces) water chestnuts, finely chopped

5 pickled jalapenos, minced

1/4 cup chopped fresh cilantro leaves

1 tablespoon salt

Lettuce or cabbage leaves to prevent rice balls from sticking

Instructions:

1. Rinse rice and soak for 3 hours.

2. Mix together all other ingredients (minus leaves) and shape into 24, 1-inch diameter, balls.

3. Cover a baking sheet with wax paper, spread rice over paper, and roll the balls in rice.

4. Cover the balls with another sheet of wax paper and refrigerate for at least an hour.

5. Place the balls on the leaves to prevent from sticking and place in the steamer bowl.

6. Steam for 30 minutes and serve hot.

Nutritional Info: Calories: 332 | Sodium: 1246 mg | Dietary Fiber: 0.8 g |
Total Fat: 6.8 g | Total Carbs: 39.5 g | Protein: 26.1 g.

Steamed and Roasted Whole Duck

Servings: 4 | Prep Time: 10 Minutes | Cook Time: 30 Minutes

Duck does not get the attention that it deserves, it is just as easy to prepare as chicken or turkey and tastes just as good.

Ingredients:

1 whole duck (4 to 5 pound)	4 cloves garlic
1 tablespoon Chinese five spice powder	1/2 bunch green onion
2 teaspoons sugar	1 tangerine, peel cut in big strips
2 teaspoons salt	1/4 cup rice vinegar
5 slices fresh ginger	1/2 cup honey
	1/2 cup soy sauce

Instructions:

1. Rinse the entire duck and pat dry with paper towels.
2. In a small bowl, mix together 5 spice, sugar, and salt.
3. Rub the mixture all over the duck inside and out.
4. Combine the ginger, garlic, green onions, and tangerine peel together and stuff into the duck cavity.
5. Fold the wing tips under the duck and tie the legs together with kitchen string.
6. Pierce the breast a few times and place in the steamer, steam for 45 minutes.
7. Combine vinegar, honey, and soy sauce in a small sauce pan and bring to a boil.
8. Reduce heat to simmer and stir for 15 minutes or until the sauce thickens.
9. Preheat oven to 375.
10. Transfer the duck to a roasting pan and glaze with the honey mixture.
11. Roast for 1 hour, glazing periodically.
12. You can cover the duck with foil if it seems like it is getting too dark.

Nutritional Info: Calories: 1350 | Sodium: 2172 mg | Dietary Fiber: 2.2 g | Total Fat: 63.8 g | Total Carbs: 49.5 g | Protein: 136.7 g.

Steamed Asian Chicken Breast

Servings: 4 | Prep Time: 40 Minutes | Cook Time: 10 Minutes

This Asian inspired recipe is nice because it brings out the flavor of the East, but is not the same old ginger and mushroom recipe.

Ingredients:

4 (7-ounce) chicken breasts

3 shallots

1 1/2 tablespoons lime juice

1 tablespoon fish sauce

1 tablespoon oyster sauce

1 teaspoon sesame oil

1 tablespoon toasted sesame seeds

Instructions:

1. Combine lime juice, fish sauce, oyster sauce, sesame oil, in a medium bowl.

2. Finely chop 1 shallot, then slice the other two diagonally.

3. Add chopped shallot to the bowl and mix well.

4. Add chicken to the bowl and coat, set aside for 30 minutes.

5. Remove chicken and place it in a steamer safe dish, pour marinade over it.

6. Place dish in steamer and steam for 10 minutes.

7. Slice chicken diagonally and serve over a bed of rice garnished with sliced shallots and sesame seeds.

Nutritional Info: Calories: 409 | Sodium: 547 mg | Dietary Fiber: 0 g |
Total Fat: 17.0 g | Total Carbs: 2.5 g | Protein: 58.3 g.

Kristin Amber

Steamed Chicken Breast with Honey Mustard Sauce

Servings: 4 | Prep Time: 10 Minutes | Cook Time: 25 Minutes

This is a simple chicken recipe that gets a huge boost when you add the honey mustard sauce.

Ingredients:

Baby potatoes, halved

Carrot slices

Broccoli florets

Zucchini slices

2 large chicken breast, thinly sliced into 4 pieces each

1 1/3 cups cream

2 tablespoons honey

1 tablespoon seeded mustard

1/2 tablespoon Dijon mustard

1 teaspoon thyme

Salt and pepper, to taste

1/2 tablespoon corn flour, see note

1 tablespoon hot water

Instructions:

1. Place the chicken in the bottom steamer bowl and cover with potatoes.

2. Sprinkle with salt and pepper.

3. Steam for 12 minutes, add the second bowl to the top with remaining vegetables and steam for another 12 minutes.

4. Add all other ingredients, except for corn flour and water, to a small sauce pan and stir over medium heat for about 5 minutes.

5. Combine flour and water and add to the sauce mix stirring for another 3 minutes or until the sauce starts to thicken.

6. Place chicken and veggies on a plate and drizzle the sauce over the chicken to serve.

Nutritional Info: Calories: 184 | Sodium: 107 mg | Dietary Fiber: 0.6 g |
Total Fat: 7.2 g | Total Carbs: 13.1 g | Protein: 17.6 g.

Steamed Chicken with Chinese Mushroom

Servings: 4 | Prep Time: 1 Hour 15 Minutes | Cook Time: 30 Minutes

This is a recipe rich in flavor, easy to throw together, and only takes a few minutes of active time.

Ingredients:

- Half of a whole chicken
- 1 handful dried wood ear mushroom
- 3 fresh shitake mushrooms, sliced
- 2 tablespoons oyster sauce
- 1 tablespoon light soy sauce
- 2 green onions, white parts
- 10 ginger sheds
- 1 teaspoon salt
- 1/2 tablespoon sesame oil

Instructions:

1. Cut the chicken into chunks and soak in water for 30 minutes, changing out the water twice in that time.
2. Mix oyster sauce, soy sauce, onions, ginger, salt, and oil together.
3. Place chicken chunks in the marinade and refrigerate for 30 minutes.
4. While the chicken marinates, soak the wood ear mushrooms and slice the shitakes.
5. Drain the wood ear mushrooms and mix all the ingredients together.
6. Transfer ingredients to the steamer and steam for 30 minutes.

Nutritional Info: Calories: 249 | Sodium: 1072 mg | Dietary Fiber: 1.7 g | Total Fat: 5.8 g | Total Carbs: 10.5 g | Protein: 37.9 g.

Light Steamed Chicken and Vegetables

Servings: 4 | Prep Time: 5 Minutes | Cook Time: 10 Minutes

This recipe is perfect if you are looking for a low-calorie meal that does not skimp on the flavor.

Ingredients:

4 (6-ounce) skinless, boneless chicken breast halves

1/4 teaspoon salt

1/4 teaspoon black pepper

3 cups (2-inch) slices asparagus

1 cup halved sugar snap peas

1/4 cup coarsely chopped fresh cilantro

1/4 cup low-sodium soy sauce

2 tablespoons rice vinegar

2 tablespoons sweet rice wine

1/2 teaspoon dark sesame oil

Instructions:

1.   Sprinkle chicken with salt and pepper.

2.   Place chicken in bottom bowl and asparagus and peas in top bowl and steam for 12 minutes.

3.   Combine cilantro and the rest of the ingredients and serve with chicken.

Nutritional Info: Calories: 271 | Sodium: 1175 mg | Dietary Fiber: 2.7 g |
Total Fat: 6.8 g | Total Carbs: 9.9 g | Protein: 41.6 g.

Steamed Chicken with Mushrooms and Dried Lily Flowers

Servings: 4 | Prep Time: 4 Hours 10 Minutes | Cook Time: 12 Minutes

This is truly a unique recipe; it is not every day that you incorporate flowers into your chicken recipe.

Ingredients:

1/4 cup dried wood ear mushrooms

1/3 cup dried lily flowers

10 medium dried shiitake mushrooms, soaked until reconstituted

1 pound boneless chicken thighs, trimmed of fat and cut into large bite-sized chunks

1/4 cup water

1 tablespoon vegetable oil

1/4 teaspoon sesame oil

1 tablespoon oyster sauce

1/4 teaspoon sugar

3/4 teaspoons salt

1/4 teaspoon freshly ground white pepper

1/2 teaspoon grated ginger

1 scallion, chopped (white and green portions divided)

1 tablespoon cornstarch

Instructions:

1. Rinse mushrooms and lilies and cut stems from both.

2. Place wood ears, shitakes, and lilies in 3 separate bowls and soak for 2 hours.

3. Chop the wood ears and slice the shitakes, drain all three.

4. In a large bowl, combine chicken, water, oils, oyster sauce, sugar, salt, pepper, ginger, and whites of scallion.

5. Mix until the chicken absorbs most of the chicken.

6. Cover the bowl and refrigerate for 2 hours.

7. Allow the mixture to return to room temperature and mix in corn starch.

8. Place chicken on a steamer safe plate and steam for 12 minutes.

Nutritional Info: Calories: 456 | Sodium: 1434 mg | Dietary Fiber: 7.8 g |
Total Fat: 12.9 g | Total Carbs: 52.9 g | Protein: 38.7 g.

Kristin Amber

8

Desserts

Cheddar Cheese Cupcakes

Servings: 6 | Prep Time: 15 Minutes | Cook Time: 15 Minutes

This unique recipe can serve as an unorthodox dessert or a midday snack.

Ingredients:

1/3 cup shredded cheddar cheese

5 tablespoons unsalted butter

1/2 cup milk

3 large eggs

1/2 cup castor sugar

Salt to taste

3/4 cups cake flour

2 teaspoons double acting baking powder

Instructions:

1. Cut butter into cubes and mix together cheese, butter, and milk.
2. Microwave the mixture in 15 second increments, stirring each time, until the ingredients are combined.
3. Mix flour and baking powder together.
4. Beat the eggs in a medium bowl until they become foamy.
5. Slowly stir in sugar until the mixture becomes creamy.
6. Add cheese mixture to creamed butter and continue to stir until ingredients are dispersed evenly.
7. Mix in the flour to create a batter, continue to mix until flour is incorporated, but there are still air bubbles.
8. Pour the mix into a muffin tin or individual cupcake wrappers.
9. Steam for 15 minutes, remove the lid and let cool for a few minutes before removing them.

Nutritional Info: Calories: 277 | Sodium: 181 mg | Dietary Fiber: 0 g | Total Fat: 14.8 g | Total Carbs: 30.7 g | Protein: 7.1 g.

Gluten Free Steamed Buns

Servings: 6 | Prep Time: 30 Minutes | Cook Time: 12 Minutes

Living a gluten free lifestyle is difficult and often you must miss out on some of the best stuff.

Ingredients:

1/4 ounce of fast-action dried yeast

2 tablespoons of water

1 teaspoon caster sugar

1/2 pint of skimmed milk, or half water, half semi-skimmed

1 1/16 ounces of unsalted butter

1/2 teaspoon salt

2 1/3 ounces of caster sugar

6 1/4 ounces of corn flour

3 ounces of potato flour

3 1/4 ounces of glutinous rice flour

3 1/2 ounces of rice flour

1 teaspoon baking powder

Instructions:

1. Mix together yeast, water, and sugar in a small bowl and set aside.

2. Combine milk and butter in a sauce pan and heat until butter is melted, then simmer.

3. Combine all dry ingredients in a large bowl and mix well.

4. Add yeast and milk to the dry ingredients and mix to form a dough.

5. Break off golf ball sized pieces of the dough and roll, then flatten and fold over.

6. Place each piece onto its own piece of parchment paper, then lay in the steamer.

7. Steam for 12 minutes.

Nutritional Info: Calories: 465 | Sodium: 393 mg | Dietary Fiber: 4.0 g |
Total Fat: 5.8 g | Total Carbs: 87.2 g | Protein: 16.1 g.

Kristin Amber

Newfoundland Molasses Duff

Servings: 8 | Prep Time: 15 Minutes | Cook Time: 2 Hours

It doesn't matter that it has a silly name, what matters is that this soft cake has an amazing flavor.

Ingredients:

1/2 cup molasses	1 1/2 teaspoons baking powder
1/2 cup butter	1/2 teaspoon baking soda
1 egg	1 teaspoon cinnamon
1 teaspoon pure vanilla extract	1/2 cup milk
1 1/2 cups flour	1 1/2 cups raisins

Instructions:

1. Spray a steamer safe basin with cooking spray.
2. Cream together the molasses and butter in a medium bowl.
3. Mix in egg and vanilla extract.
4. In a separate bowl combine flour, powder, soda, and cinnamon.
5. Mix dry ingredients and milk into the molasses slowly alternating between the two as you go.
6. Add the raisins and continue to stir until raisins are dispersed evenly.
7. Pour the batter into the basin and place in the steamer.
8. Steam for 2 hours, be aware that you will need to reset the timer and add water during the process.

Nutritional Info: Calories: 287 | Sodium: 180 mg | Dietary Fiber: 1.8 g |
Total Fat: 12.7 g | Total Carbs: 41.0 g | Protein: 4.6 g.

Steamed Chocolate Banana Cupcakes

Servings: 7 | Prep Time: 10 Minutes | Cook Time: 15 Minutes

This and many other recipes are going to blow your mind when it comes to steaming desserts.

Ingredients:

2 large eggs

55 grams brown sugar

45 grams low protein flour

20 grams cocoa powder

1 teaspoon double acting baking powder

2 tablespoons olive oil

1 medium size banana, mashed

Instructions:

1. Mix flour, coco powder, and baking powder and set the bowl aside.

2. Beat the eggs in a large bowl until they become frothy.

3. Add brown sugar to the eggs and mix until creamy.

4. Stir in olive oil.

5. Slowly pour in the flour mix, stirring as you go.

6. Mash the banana and add it to the bowl, mixing until evenly dispersed.

7. Pour the batter into a line cupcake mold that will fit in the steamer.

8. Steam for 12 minutes, remove the lid and allow to cool for a few minutes before you remove the cupcakes.

Nutritional Info: Calories: 130 | Sodium: 24 mg | Dietary Fiber: 1.5 g | Total Fat: 5.9 g | Total Carbs: 18.5 g | Protein: 3.2 g.

Kristin Amber

Steamed Chocolate Lava Cake

Servings: 3 | Prep Time: 10 Minutes | Cook Time: 8 Minutes

This one goes without saying, it is the kind of desert that dreams are made of.

Ingredients:

85g good quality dark chocolate

45 grams unsalted butter

1 1/2 whole eggs

1 1/2 egg yolks

35 grams castor sugar

22 grams all-purpose flour

Salt to taste

1/2 teaspoon vanilla essence

Instructions:

1. Brush 3 (6-ounce) ramekins with butter and sprinkle with castor sugar.

2. Break the chocolate apart, then combine it with butter in a steamer safe bowl.

3. Steam until the chocolate is melted, set aside to cool slightly.

4. Combine eggs and sugar into a medium bowl.

5. Mix in flour and salt, then add the chocolate and vanilla essence; continue to stir until smooth.

6. Pour batter into ramekins and steam for 9 minutes.

Nutritional Info: Calories: 390 | Sodium: 144 mg | Dietary Fiber: 1.2 g |
Total Fat: 25.1 g | Total Carbs: 34.7 g | Protein: 7.2 g.

Steamed Green Tea Cakes

Servings: 4 | Prep Time: 10 Minutes | Cook Time 15 Minutes

This recipe is easy to throw together and has a great flavor for breakfast or dessert.

Ingredients:

1 large egg	1 1/2 tablespoons sugar
1 tablespoon vegetable oil	1/2 cup all-purpose flour
1 tablespoon honey	1 teaspoon baking powder
3 tablespoons plain regular yogurt	1 teaspoon green tea powder

Instructions:

1. Mix together egg and oil in a medium bowl.
2. Add honey and yogurt to the bowl and mix thoroughly.
3. Mix in the sugar until it is completely dissolved.
4. Sift together flour and baking powder, then mix it into the egg mixture.
5. Pour in the green tea powder and stir until even.
6. Line 4 steamer safe ramekins with cupcake liners and pour even amount of tea mixture into each one.
7. Steam for 14 Minutes.

Nutritional Info: Calories: 147 | Sodium: 27 mg | Dietary Fiber: 0 g |
Total Fat: 4.9 g | Total Carbs: 22.3 g | Protein: 3.9 g.

Kristin Amber

Lemon Steamed Pudding

Servings: 4 | Prep Time: 15 Minutes | Cook Time: 40 Minutes

This may be one of my favorite desserts. I am a huge fan of anything citrus, and this pudding recipe brings out all the flavor of lemon without the sour.

Ingredients:

2 large eggs, separated

1/2 cup granulated sugar, plus more for the ramekins

3 tablespoons plus 1 teaspoon all-purpose flour

Salt to taste

2/3 cups buttermilk

2 1/2 tablespoons fresh lemon juice

Finely chopped zest of 1 1/2 lemons

Instructions:

1. Preheat the oven to 300 degrees.

2. Butter and sugar 4, 4 ounce ramekins and place them in the oven.

3. Beat the egg whites and sift the sugar, flour, and salt together.

4. Combine lemon juice, buttermilk, egg yolks, and lemon zest in a medium bowl.

5. Slowly add in flour mix and egg whites then stir until the mixture is smooth.

6. Remove ramekins from the oven and pour pudding evenly into each ramekin.

7. Steam for about 40 minutes or until the pudding sets.

Nutritional Info: Calories: 176 | Sodium: 80 mg | Dietary Fiber: 0.9 g | Total Fat: 3.1 g | Total Carbs: 34.0 g | Protein: 5.4 g.

Steamed Jam Pudding

Servings: 4 | Prep Time: 15 Minutes | Cook Time 1 Hour 30 Minutes

Desserts like this are why I love having a steamer, it can cook just about anything, even delicious pudding.

Ingredients:

1/4 cup jam

1 1/8 stick butter

1 teaspoon vanilla essence

1/2 cup caster sugar

2 eggs

2 cups self-rising flour

1/2 cup milk

Instructions:

1. Spread jam over the bottom of a steamer safe basin.
2. Cream butter, essence, and sugar together.
3. Beat in eggs one at a time.
4. Mix in flour and milk slowly.
5. Pour over jam and place in the steamer.
6. It takes about 1 1/2 hours to steam so you will need to return to the steamer to reset the time/fill the water.
7. The pudding is ready when it solidifies.

Nutritional Info: Calories: 654 | Sodium: 236 mg | Dietary Fiber: 1.9 g |
Total Fat: 29.2 g | Total Carbs: 88.3 g | Protein: 10.6 g.

Kristin Amber

Steamed Jackfruit Cakes

Servings: 4 - 5 | Prep Time: 10 Minutes | Cook Time: 20 Minutes

Jackfruit is increasing in popularity in the United States and with recipes like this one you will see why. This recipe does have some unique ingredients in it so take inventory before you start.

Ingredients:

1 cup jack fruit flesh	1/2 teaspoon cardamom powder
1/2 cup grated coconut	Water as required
1/2 cup jaggery, grated	12 – 15 bay leaves
1 cup rice flour	Salt to taste

Instructions:

1. Mince Jackfruit flesh and place in a large bowl.
2. Add coconut, rice flour, jaggery, cardamom, and salt.
3. Add water a little at a time and knead into a sticky dough.
4. For a bay leaf into a cone and secure it using a toothpick.
5. Pour in Jackfruit dough and fold the top of the leaf over to close.
6. Steam for 20 Minutes.

Nutritional Info: Calories: 349 | Sodium: 1442 mg | Dietary Fiber: 3.6 g | Total Fat: 4.4 g | Total Carbs: 75.5 g | Protein: 3.7 g.

Steamed Latte Cake

Servings: 5 | Prep Time: 5 Minutes | Cook Time: 15 Minutes

It only takes a few ingredients to make a family pleasing desert that is super simple to make.

Ingredients:

1 1/3 ounces flour	1/2 ounce matcha (latte powder, 1 stick)
1 ounce granulated sugar	
2/3 cups warm water	

Instructions:

1. Mix all ingredients together in a medium bowl.
2. Pour mixture into 5 steamer safe ramekins or a muffin tin.
3. Steam for 14 minutes.

Nutritional Info: Calories: 7 | Sodium: 26 mg | Dietary Fiber: 0.6 g | Total Fat: 0 g | Total Carbs: 1.6 g | Protein: 0 g.

Steamed Lemon Custard with Raspberries

Servings: 2 | Prep Time: 10 Minutes | Cook Time: 20 Minutes

This heavenly desert is easy to throw together and has the perfect portion size.

Ingredients:

2 large egg whites

1/4 teaspoon cream of tartar

1/2 lemon, zested and juiced

1/4 teaspoon pure vanilla extract

3 tablespoons cake flour

1/4 cup sugar

1/4 teaspoon salt

20 fresh raspberries, plus more for garnish

Fresh mint leaves, for garnish

Confectioners' sugar, for dusting

Instructions:

1. Beat the egg whites in a large bowl until they become frothy.

2. Add the cream of tartar, lemon juice, zest, and extract and continue to beat.

3. Combine flour, sugar, and salt and mix with the egg whites.

4. Place 10 raspberries on the bottom of 2 (6-ounce) ramekins.

5. Pour the batter over the ramekins.

6. Place ramekins in the steamer and steam for 20 minutes.

7. Garnish with raspberries, mint, and confectioners' sugar.

Nutritional Info: Calories: 250 | Sodium: 298 mg | Dietary Fiber: 13.4 g |
Total Fat: 1.6 g | Total Carbs: 59.5 g | Protein: 3.9 g.

Steamed Tapioca and Red Bean Cakes

Servings: 12 | Prep Time: 1 Hour 10 Minutes | Cook Time: 25 Minutes

This recipe is so unique, so easy, and so delicious that you won't believe it until you try it.

Ingredients:

200 grams tapioca pearls

85 grams sugar

1 tablespoon olive oil

145 grams sweetened red bean paste

Instructions:

1. Soak tapioca pearls for at least an hour.

2. Rinse and drain pearls, mix in oil and sugar, then set aside.

3. Grease a mini-muffin tin that will fit in your steamer.

4. Spoon a tablespoon of tapioca into each cup.

5. Add bean paste to each cup. Top with more pearl mix & Steam for 25 Minutes.

Nutritional Info: Calories: 109 | Sodium: 0 mg | Dietary Fiber: 0 g |
Total Fat: 1.2 g | Total Carbs: 24.2 g | Protein: 0.6 g.

Thai-Style Steamed Tapioca Cake

Servings: 8 | Prep Time: 10 Minutes | Cook Time: 20 Minutes

This creamy cake is not like anything that you are used to, and that is a good thing.

Ingredients:

1 cup white sugar

1/4 cup unsweetened coconut cream

1 tablespoon cornstarch

4 1/2 cups grated, peeled yucca root
(tapioca root)

1 cup water

2 cups flaked coconut, divided

1/4 teaspoon salt

Instructions:

1. Mix the sugar, cream, and cornstarch together until sugar dissolves.

2. Add cassava, water, and 1/3 of flaked coconut.

3. Toss the remaining flakes with salt in a separate bowl and set aside.

4. Pour the mixture into 8, 1 cup, steamer safe, ramekins.

5. Sprinkle a little coconut salt mixture over each ramekin & Steam for 20 minutes.

Nutritional Info: Calories: 371 | Sodium: 96 mg | Dietary Fiber: 4.1 g |
Total Fat: 8.8 g | Total Carbs: 73.5 g | Protein: 2.4 g.

Kristin Amber

CHAPTER

9

Steamed
Rice Recipes

Herb Steamed Rice

Servings: 4 | Prep Time: 15 Minutes | Cook Time: 30 Minutes

This is a quintessential rice recipe that is perfect to serve with almost any dish.

Ingredients:

3 tablespoons unsalted butter

1 medium onion, diced

1 cup long-grain white rice, rinsed and drained

1 garlic clove, minced

1 1/2 cups water

Salt to taste

1/4 cup chopped mixed herbs, such as parsley, chives and tarragon

Instructions:

1. Add butter and onion to a saucepan over medium heat and sauté for 5 minutes.

2. Stir in rice and garlic, then add water and salt. Cook for 10 minutes.

3. Drain rice, stir in herbs, and transfer to the steamer to steam for 30 minutes.

4. Serve warm.

Nutritional Info: Calories: 263 | Sodium: 68 mg | Dietary Fiber: 2.1 g | Total Fat: 9.1 g | Total Carbs: 41.1 g | Protein: 4.0 g.

Steamed Rice Cakes

Servings: 6 | Prep Time: 2 Hours 10 Minutes | Cook Time: 20 Minutes

This is another great snack that takes a little time to prepare, but the family will love.

Ingredients:

9 ounces water milled rice flour

2 ounces plain flour

5 ounces sugar

210 ml-220 ml hot water

1 1/2 teaspoons instant yeast

Oil, for brushing

Instructions:

1. Dissolve the sugar into hot water and set aside to cool to room temperature.

2. Mix flours and yeast together, then combine with sugar water and set aside for at least 2 hours—batter should double in size.

3. Scoop batter into a steamer safe mold and steam for 20 minutes.

4. Serve warm, these can easily be reheated if necessary.

Nutritional Info: Calories: 282 | Sodium: 2 mg | Dietary Fiber: 1.5 g | Total Fat: 0.7 g | Total Carbs: 65.3 g | Protein: 3.9 g.

Steamed Rice and Spring Vegetables with Fried Eggs

Servings: 2 | Prep Time: 55 Minutes | Cook Time: 15 Minutes

The rice kind of takes a back seat in this recipe, but if it wasn't for the rice this recipe would be nothing.

Ingredients:

- 2 scallions, chopped, whites and greens separated
- 1 1/4 cups long-grain brown rice
- 1 tablespoon reduced-sodium soy sauce
- 2 teaspoons grated ginger
- 1/2 teaspoon toasted sesame oil
- 2 heads baby bok choy, chopped
- 1 cup peas
- 2 teaspoons olive oil
- 4 large eggs
- Kosher salt and freshly ground black pepper
- 1/4 cup chopped fresh cilantro

Instructions:

1. Combine rice, sesame oil, scallion whites, ginger, and 2 cups water, mix well and bring to a boil.

2. Reduce heat and simmer for 40 minutes.

3. Add veggies to a large bowl and mix together with rice mix.

4. Transfer to your rice mixture to the steamer and steam for 5 minutes.

5. Heat oil in a medium to large skillet and fry eggs until the whites are solid, but the yolks are runny.

6. Lay eggs over rice and veggies and season with salt, pepper, and cilantro.

Nutritional Info: Calories: 807 | Sodium: 1149 mg | Dietary Fiber: 16.9 g |
Total Fat: 21.0 g | Total Carbs: 123.1 g | Protein: 39.0 g.

Kristin Amber

Steamed Sticky Rice Cake with Coconut Filling

Servings: 6 | Prep Time: 1 hour 30 minutes | Cook Time: 25 Minutes

This is a delicious recipe that is perfect for a small and unique desert, it does take a little time so be prepared.

Ingredients:

9 ounces sticky rice flour

1/2 teaspoon salt

2 tablespoons sugar

Hot water

4 ounces icing sugar

1/2 cup water

5 ounces coconut meat (smashed)

1/2 bowl roasted peanut

1 tablespoon tapioca starch

Banana leaves

Instructions:

1. Mix together rice flour, salt, and sugar.
2. Slowly pour in hot water while stirring until the mixture becomes soft and smooth.
3. Knead by hand for about 5 minutes.
4. Place peanuts in a pan over medium heat and smash them.
5. Mix in icing sugar and 1/2 cup water and cook until mixture begins to darken.
6. Add coconut meat to the pan and cook for another 10 minutes.
7. Add tapioca starch and a pinch of salt, then reduce heat.
8. Role leaves into cone shapes.
9. Cut off chunks of dough roll and flatten them.
10. Roll rice mixture into balls and lay in the center of your flattened dough.
11. Place each ball in the leaves, rice side down.
12. Steam for 25 minutes.

Nutritional Info: Calories: 471 | Sodium: 204 mg | Dietary Fiber: 5.2 g |
Total Fat: 20.5 g | Total Carbs: 65.8 g | Protein: 9.6 g.

Steamed Rice Rolls

Servings: 4 | Prep Time: 1 Hour 5 Minutes | Cook Time: 4 Minutes

This is an awesome recipe to make a quick grab and go snack.

Ingredients:

5 ounces rice flour

1 1/2 tablespoons wheat starch

2 tablespoons corn flour

1 tablespoon corn oil

2 cups water

1/2 teaspoon salt

Instructions:

1. Combine flours and starch in a large bowl.

2. Slowly add the water while stirring.

3. Add the oil and salt and mix until smooth.

4. Cover and leave for one hour.

5. Pour 1/4 cup of batter onto a steamer safe plate or another dish that allows for a thin layer.

6. Steam for 4 minutes.

7. Roll the flat layer into a roll, repeat with the rest of the batter.

Nutritional Info: Calories: 193 | Sodium: 294 mg | Dietary Fiber: 1.1 g |
Total Fat: 4.1 g | Total Carbs: 36.0 g | Protein: 2.4 g.

Kristin Amber

Yaki Onigiri with Sweet Potato and Avocado Filling

Servings: 12 | Prep Time: 50 Minutes | Cook Time: 8 Minutes

These are awesome for a snack but will make you the talk of the party if you serve them as an appetizer.

Ingredients:

1 1/2 cups brown sushi rice	1/2 teaspoon salt
3 cups water	1/2 – 1 small sweet potato
1/4 cup sesame seeds	1 teaspoon toasted sesame oil
2 tablespoons rice wine vinegar	1/2 avocado
1 tablespoon sugar	Olive oil for frying

Instructions:

1. Rinse the rice and prepare as per the instructions on the bag.
2. Drain any excess water from the rice and return it to pot.
3. Mix vinegar, sugar, and salt in a small bowl and pour it over the rice.
4. Add steamed seeds and mix well.
5. Peel sweet potatoes and slice them thinly, lay them in the steamer and steam for 12 minutes.
6. Peel and slice avocado.
7. Line a measuring cup with parchment paper and press 1 tablespoon of rice into it.
8. Lay down one slice of sweet potato and one slice of avocado.
9. Cover with a little more rice.
10. Lift the parchment papers out of the cup and form the rice into a ball.
11. Heat some oil in a pan and add rice balls roll around for about 8 minutes.
12. Serve immediately for best results.

Nutritional Info: Calories: 132 | Sodium: 102 mg | Dietary Fiber: 1.4 g |
Total Fat: 3.7 g | Total Carbs: 21.9 g | Protein: 2.4 g.

Pantry

- **POTATOES** – There are so many things you can do with steamed potatoes you could almost make a cook book just about them. Steaming a potato may be the best way to cook them (sorry baked potato).

- **RICE** – Dry rice will stay for a lifetime, which is spectacular for those looking to save money. Steaming it is also super easy which makes this the perfect food to keep in your pantry.

- **DRIED HERBS** – These are important to keep in the kitchen no matter what kind of cooking you are doing. Adding a few of these to the water or rubbing them on your meats can bring out an entirely new flavor profile.

- **LEMONS AND LIMES** – Much like herbs, adding the juice or rinds of lemons and limes to your water or in the bowls themselves can enhance the flavor profile and completely change the taste of the dish.

- **WHITE AND RED ONION** – There is definitely a theme here. These pungent vegetables can take an ordinary dish to an extraordinary dish.

- **WHITE AND RED WINE** – It never hurts to keep an extra bottle or two of wine on hand for any occasion. Adding either of these wines to a recipe is a sure fire way to take the recipe to the next level.

UMAMI *Fifth flavor*

Often called the "fifth flavor" after sweet, salty, sour, and bitter, umami can best be described as savory, but what does savory taste like? In Japanese, umami translates to "a pleasant savory taste." Scientifically, umami is determined by the amount of glutamate in a particular food. (Think of it as a natural way of getting a flavor boost similar to MSG). The amazing thing about umami is that it can be found in all kinds of foods. Try adding a pinch of one of these ingredients to almost any recipe. **Often the taste is amazing!**

Vegetables/Plants

Seaweed
(kombu and nori)

Soybean products
(Soy sauce, miso, tofu)

Tomatoes

Green teas

Kimchi
(Korean fermented vegetables)

Mushrooms

Meats

Bacon

Ham

Pork

Beef

Chicken

Eggs

Seafood

Sardines

Bonito
(Dried fish flakes)

Tuna

Mackerel

Shrimp

Anchovies

Oysters

Mussels

Caviar and
other fish eggs

Cheeses

Parmesan

Comte/Gruyere

Roquefort

Gouda

Cheddar

Flavor Building

The best way to start building flavors is with a general seasoning with salt and black pepper. You can also experiment with these herbs and spices to build fun, new flavors with different proteins.

BEEF
Shallots
Garlic
Thyme
Cumin
Rosemary
Red Wine

SALMON
Lemon Pepper
Citrus
Paprika
Dill
Basil
Olive Oil

PORK
Mustard
Thyme
White Wine
Apple Cider
Rosemary

CHICKEN
Rosemary
Garlic
White Wine
Thyme
Soy Sauce
Lemon Pepper
Olive Oil

VEGETABLES
Olive Oil
Thyme
Mint
Onion Powder

Wine and Beer Pairing

Try these varieties with your favorite meats and fish.

NEW YORK OR RIBEYE STEAKS

Wine	Beer
Cabernet Sauvignon	IPA
Malbec	Brown Ale
Shiraz	Stout

SALMON

Wine	Beer
Sauvignon Blanc	Pilsner
Pinot Grigio	Lager
Riesling	IPA

PORK

Wine	Beer
Chardonnay	Brown Ale
Pinot Noir	IPA
	Stout

WHITE FISHES

Wine	Beer
Sauvignon Blanc	Light Ale
Chardonnay	Pilsner
	Hefeweissen

CHICKEN

Wine	Beer
Sauvignon Blanc	Pilsner
Merlot	Lager
Pinot Noir	Light Ale

10 CLASSIC *Salad Dressings*

Ranch
 mayonnaise | buttermilk | chives | dill | onion powder | garlic powder | salt | black pepper

Caesar
 canola oil | parmesan cheese | anchovy | fresh garlic | egg yolk | black pepper

Bleu Cheese
 blue cheese | buttermilk | sour cream | mayonnaise | white wine vinegar | sugar | garlic powder | black pepper

Thousand Islands
 mayonnaise | ketchup | white vinegar | sugar | sweet pickle relish | salt | black pepper

Italian
 olive oil | white or red wine vinegar | garlic powder | oregano | dried basil | onion powder | crushed red pepper | salt | black pepper | lemon juice

Balsamic Vinaigrette
 balsamic vinegar | honey | dijon mustard | olive oil | garlic | salt | black pepper

Honey Mustard
 dijon mustard | honey | apple cider vinegar | salt | vegetable oil

Greek
 red wine vinegar | olive oil | lemon juice | dried oregano | salt | black pepper

French
 vegetable oil | ketchup | sugar | white vinegar | water | garlic powder | salt | black pepper

Russian
 onion | mayonnaise | ketchup | horseradish | hot sauce | worcestershire sauce | paprika | salt

10 CLASSIC *Sauces*

Bordelaise
 red wine   shallots   dried thyme   bay leaf   beef stock   salt   black pepper

Hollandaise
 egg yolks   lemon juice   butter   salt

Mayonnaise
 egg yolks   dry mustard   sugar   lemon juice   white wine vinegar   vegetable oil   salt

Buffalo
 Hot sauce (like Frank's Red Hot)   butter   vinegar   Worcestershire sauce   garlic powder

Italian Tomato
 tomatoes   onions   garlic   olive oil   basil   oregano   salt   black pepper

Chimichurri
 fresh parsley   garlic   oregano   olive oil   white wine vinegar   salt   black pepper

Salsa Verde
 tomatillos   onion   serrano chile   garlic   cilantro   vegetable oil   salt

Alfredo
 butter   heavy cream   garlic   Parmesan cheese   parsley

Bechamel
 milk   butter   flour   salt

Barbecue
 ketchup   apple juice   apple cider vinegar   brown sugar   butter   chili powder   garlic   onion   salt

A FUNCTIONAL PANTRY:

If you are going to cook a wide variety of dishes, you will need to have certain ingredients on-hand at all times. Keep your pantry well stocked with these ingredients:

All-purpose flour: Good for general baking and other kitchen uses

Baking powder: A double acting leavening agent that is needed for most baking

Baking soda: A leavening agent that is used when there are acidic ingredients

Kosher salt: less harsh tasting than table salt and good for cooking

Black pepper: used for seasoning before and after cooking

Olive oil: flavorful and good for low-temperature cooking and salad dressings

Vinegars: white, apple cider, white wine, red wine, and balsamic

Baking chocolate: good for a variety of desserts

Vanilla extract: flavorful addition to baked goods

White sugar: needed for most types of baking

Brown sugar: needed for many types of cakes, cookies, as well as savory dishes

Honey: a great natural sweetener

Long grain white rice: great as a light side dish

Brown rice: a healthier alternative to white rice

Breadcrumbs: handy for baking and frying

Stocks: chicken, beef, and vegetable for sauces, stews, and additional flavor

Beans: high in protein and fiber and useful in many dishes

Dry herbs and spices: bay leaves, cayenne pepper, chili powder, cinnamon, cloves, crushed red pepper, cumin, curry powder, fennel seed, garlic, ginger, nutmeg, oregano, paprika (sweet and smoked), rosemary, thyme

Dairy: milk, salted and unsalted butter, eggs, plain yogurt

Cheeses: cheddar, Parmesan, goat cheese, low moisture mozzarella

HOW TO CHOOSE VEGETABLES:

Leafy greens
Look for greens that are green all over. Otherwise, they may be starting to rot.

Tomatoes
Avoid bruised or discolored tomatoes. Tomatoes sold on the vine typically last longer than those sold without the vine.

Potatoes
Avoid potatoes that have a slight greenish hue. Look for potatoes that do not have any deep scars or large bruises.

Carrots
Look for carrots that have a healthy orange color and fresh-looking greens.

Peppers
Peppers should be free from bruises and their skin should be smooth and not wrinkly. Also look for healthy looking stems.

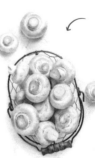

Mushrooms
Look for firm, fresh, smooth appearance. If the cap is closed underneath the flavor will be delicate. If it is open and you can see the gills it will have richer flavor. Fresh herbs: Herbs will last longer if they have the roots attached. After buying fresh herbs, put them in a glass of water to help them stay fresh longer.

HOW TO CHOOSE MEATS:

Beef

Most beef is either "choice" or "prime." Prime has the highest fat content, but it is also very expensive. If you can afford prime, it's the best, but most choice beef is quite good as well. When shopping for beef, look for marbling (the more the better) and try to find beef that has a healthy red color.

Grain fed or grass fed?
Most beef in the United States is grain fed, and this is what Americans are used to eating. Grass fed beef has a stronger flavor and often a higher fat content. A lot of grass-fed beef is grain fed and then finished on grass.

Pork

Pork comes in many varieties, and again, freshness is key. Pork chops should be a light pink color with small ribbons of fat through the meat. Always look for well-marbled pork. When buying pork loins and tenderloins, look for pieces that have been well trimmed. Otherwise, you end up paying for fat you will throw away. When buying bacon, avoid those containing a lot of sugar in the dry rub.

Fresh fish

Fresh fish—meaning it has not been frozen—is always better. It will have a better texture and fresher flavor. When buying salmon, look for fish with high fat content. This will make the meat juicier. Also, make sure your salmon has a sweet smell and not a fishy smell. Ahi tuna should be deep red in color and should have almost no smell at all. Also, look for well-trimmed tuna that has had the bloodline removed. White fishes like flounder, halibut, cod, and sole should have a slightly sweet smell and slick, not dry, looking flesh.

Chicken

When buying chicken, it's all about freshness. Fresh chicken should have very little smell and the skin should be a healthy yellowish color. Commercial chicken is often pre-brined, meaning it has been injected with salt water. While brining a chicken before cooking is a great way to improve flavor and moisture, avoid pre-brined chicken because you will end up paying for water. Also avoid chicken raised with any kind of hormones. When selecting a whole chicken, try to find one that is between four and five pounds for best flavor and texture.

Shellfish

Avoid buying frozen shellfish. It will have a mushy texture and slightly sulfurous smell. When buying oysters, try to buy local because oysters are sold live. For lobsters and crabs, live-bought is best. Otherwise, they can have a fishy smell. Pre-cooked lobsters and crab often become overcooked when reheated.

WAYS TO COOK *Vegetables*

WAYS TO COOK *Meat*

ASPARAGUS

Steam	Roast at	Grill
10 min	350 - 10 min	5 min

NY STEAK/RIBEYE

Broil	Grill
4 min per side	4 min per side

CARROTS

Steam	Roast at	Grill
15 min	350 - 20 min	10 min

FILET MIGNON

Broil	Grill
5 min per side	5-6 min per side

POTATOES

Steam	Roast at	Grill
20 min	350 - 40 min	15 min

TRI TIP

Roast at	Grill
375 - 40 min	25-30 min

ZUCCHINI

Steam	Roast at	Grill
10 min	350 - 20 min	10 min

CHICKEN (WHOLE)

Roast at	Grill
375 - 90 min	90 min

BELL PEPPERS

Steam	Roast at	Grill
5 min	350 - 10 min	5 min

CHICKEN (BREAST)

Sautee	Grill
8 min per side	5-6 min per side

GREEN BEANS

Steam	Roast at	Grill
5 min	350 - 15 min	Do not grill

CHICKEN (THIGHS)

Roast at	Grill
375 - 30 min	15-20 min

BROCCOLI

Steam	Roast at	Grill
10 min	350 - 15 min	10 min

PORK CHOPS

Sautee	Grill
5 min per side	5 min per side

CAULIFLOWER

Steam	Roast at	Grill
10 min	350 - 15 min	10 min

PORK TENDERLOIN

Roast at	Grill
350 - 20 min	12-15 min

HOW LONG DOES FOOD LAST IN THE FREEZER? (RAW UNLESS STATED OTHERWISE)

Meat, poultry, eggs & seafood

Beef/Lamb/Pork	4 to 12 months
Ham (cooked)	1 to 2 months
Ham	6 months
Chicken/turkey	9 months
Eggs	DO NOT FREEZE EGGS
Chicken nuggets	1 to 3 months
Hamburger patties	3 to 4 months
Hot dogs	1 to 2 months
Lean fish	6 months
Fatty fish	2 to 3 months
Shellfish	3 to 6 months

Produce

Fruit (except bananas)	10 to 12 months
Bananas	3 months
Citrus fruit	4 to 6 months
Most vegetables	8 to 10 months
Tomatoes	2 months

Dairy

Ice Cream	1 to 2 months
Butter	6 to 9 months

Other

Soup/stew	2 to 3 months
Fruit juice	8 to 12 months
Cake	4 to 6 months
Cookies (baked)	3 months
Cookie dough	2 months
Pies (baked)	2 to 4 months
Pies (unbaked)	8 months

KITCHEN UNIT CONVERSION

1 teaspoon = 1/3 tbsp = 4.9 ml

1 dessertspoon = 2 tsp = 9.9 ml

1 tablespoon = 1.5 dstsp / 3 tsp = 14.8 ml

1 fuid ounce = 2 tbsp / 6 tsp = 29.6 ml

1 cup = 16 tbsp / 48 tsp = 236.6 ml

1 quart = 4 cup = 946 ml

1 gal = 4 quart / 16 cup = 3.79 l

1 ounce = 2 tbsp = 28.4 g

1 pounds = 16 oz = 453.6 g

Made in the USA
Columbia, SC
24 August 2024

41064530R00072